Mariella Moretti

SCHNELLKURS ENGLISCH

Mariella Moretti

SCHNELLKURS ENGLISCH

Weltbild Verlag

Koordination
Carla Tanzi
Beratung
Michel Langrognet
Grafische Gestaltung
Maurizio Bejetti
Illustrationen
Severino Baraldi
Barbara Battiston (M.I.A.)
Marco D'Aponte (M.I.A.)
Gloria Fava (M.I.A.)
Alessandro Fedini
Ezio Giglioli
Gabriele Pozzi
Aldo Ripamonti
Mario Russo
Franco Spaliviero
Reproduktionskontrolle
Silvano Caldara
Druck und Bindung
Gruppo Editoriale Fabbri, Milano
Deutsche Ausgabe
topic Verlag GmbH
Karlsfeld bei München

EINLEITUNG

Eine Fremdsprache beherrscht bekanntlich, wer über einen großen Wortschatz verfügt. Das heißt aber nicht nur, Wörter zu erkennen und zu verstehen (passiver Wortschatz), sondern auch sie in den Situationen des Alltags sowie im persönlichen Gespräch und in der Schriftform korrekt anzuwenden (aktiver Wortschatz).

Mit diesem Bildwörterbuch hat der Jugendliche zwischen neun und fünfzehn Jahren die einzigartige Möglichkeit, die einzelnen Begriffe über das Bild zu erfassen. So wird das Einprägen von neuen Worten wesentlich vereinfacht. Abstraktes Auswendiglernen wird dadurch vermieden, daß die Wörter in ganzen Redewendungen und typischen Situationen begegnen.

Wesentlicher Bestandteil dieses Werks sind die beiden Sprachkassetten. Sie enthalten sämtliche Dialoge des Buchs und sind im „englischen Originalton" gesprochen. Es wird unbedingt empfohlen, beim Abspielen der Kassetten die Texte im Buch zu lesen und laut mitzusprechen. So gelangt man am schnellsten zur korrekten Aussprache des Englischen. Die Arbeit mit den Kassetten sollte häufig wiederholt werden.

Mit dem Werk erarbeitet man einen aktiven Wortschatz, der weit über die Mindestanforderungen des Straßburger Threshold Level hinausgeht. Sämtliche Standardsituationen des Alltags sowie im Schul- und Familienleben werden berücksichtigt. Auch hilft eine Reihe von Wortspielen beim Erlernen des neuen Wortschatzes.

Das alphabetisch geordnete Wörterverzeichnis Englisch-Deutsch und Deutsch-Englisch im Anhang des Buches erleichtert das Nachschlagen des gelernten Vokabulars.

INHALT

BEGLEITKASSETTEN

Die zu diesem Bildwörterbuch gehörigen Kassetten enthalten alle darin verzeichneten Redewendungen. Das am Anfang zu hörende Leitmotiv wird bei jedem Themawechsel wiederholt.

Hallo, this is your cassette with the phrases from your book.
When you hear this,  it means a change of subject.

THAT'S ME

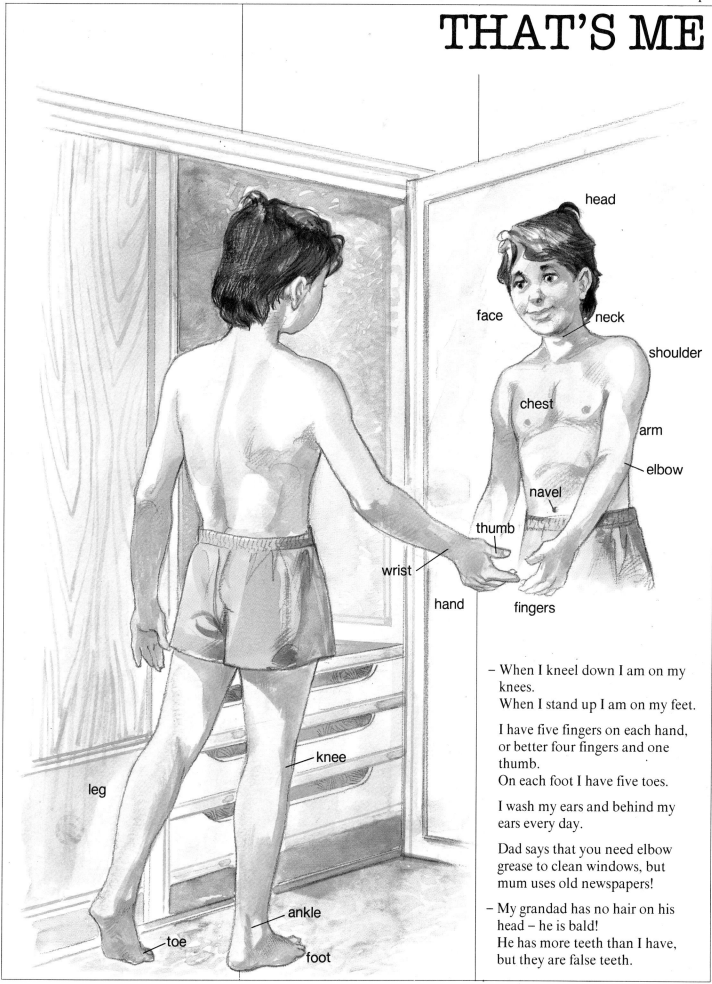

head

face

neck

shoulder

chest

arm

elbow

navel

thumb

wrist

hand

fingers

knee

leg

ankle

toe

foot

– When I kneel down I am on my knees.
When I stand up I am on my feet.

I have five fingers on each hand, or better four fingers and one thumb.
On each foot I have five toes.

I wash my ears and behind my ears every day.

Dad says that you need elbow grease to clean windows, but mum uses old newspapers!

– My grandad has no hair on his head – he is bald!
He has more teeth than I have, but they are false teeth.

THE HUMAN BODY

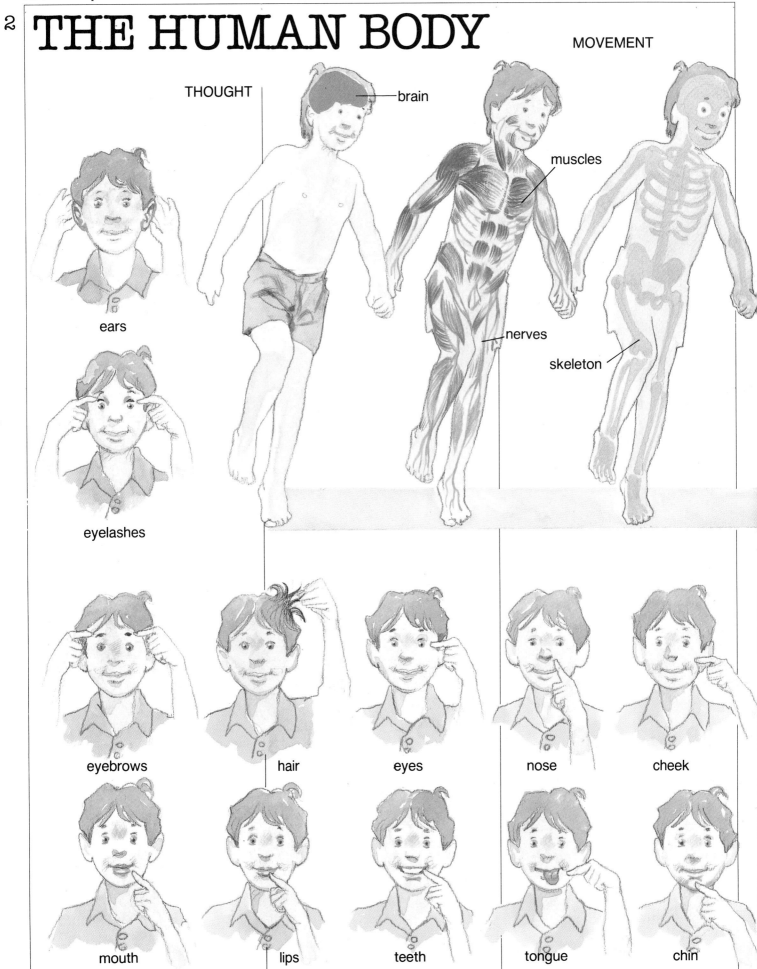

THOUGHT

MOVEMENT

brain

muscles

nerves

skeleton

ears

eyelashes

eyebrows

hair

eyes

nose

cheek

mouth

lips

teeth

tongue

chin

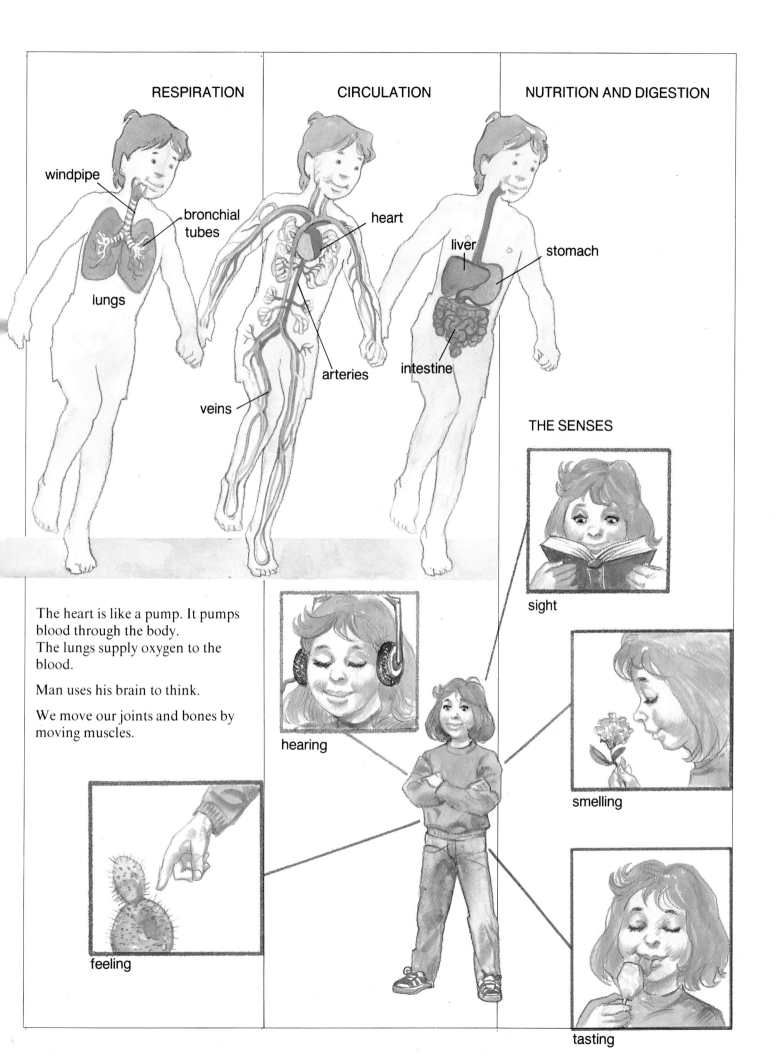

RESPIRATION

windpipe

bronchial tubes

lungs

CIRCULATION

heart

arteries

veins

NUTRITION AND DIGESTION

liver

stomach

intestine

THE SENSES

sight

hearing

smelling

The heart is like a pump. It pumps blood through the body.
The lungs supply oxygen to the blood.

Man uses his brain to think.

We move our joints and bones by moving muscles.

feeling

tasting

3 FEELINGS

- James is *frightened*. He says he has just seen a ghost at the garden gate.

- George won the football pools last week. He's so *generous* that he has given most of the money to charity.

- Ann says her younger sister is much prettier than she is. She admits that she has always been *jealous* of her.

- No one wants to play with Tom. He's a *selfish* boy; he always wants the biggest slice of cake. He always wants to win every game.

happy

sad

generous

jealous

proud

frightened

angry

selfish

IMPORTANT MOMENTS

BIRTH

mother

newborn baby

- I remember my little sister's christening.
  She cried and cried when the water was poured on her head.

- When are you making your First Communion?
- On the 14th of June.

- Why weren't you at school yesterday?
- My uncle got married and I went to the wedding.

- I had never been to a funeral until my grandfather died.

CHRISTENING

godfather

godmother

robes

priest

child to be baptized

font basin

crucifix

communion cup

Host

FIRST COMMUNION

WEDDING

bridegroom

bride

ring

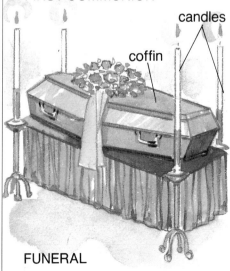

candles

coffin

FUNERAL

5 FAMILY RELATIONSHIPS

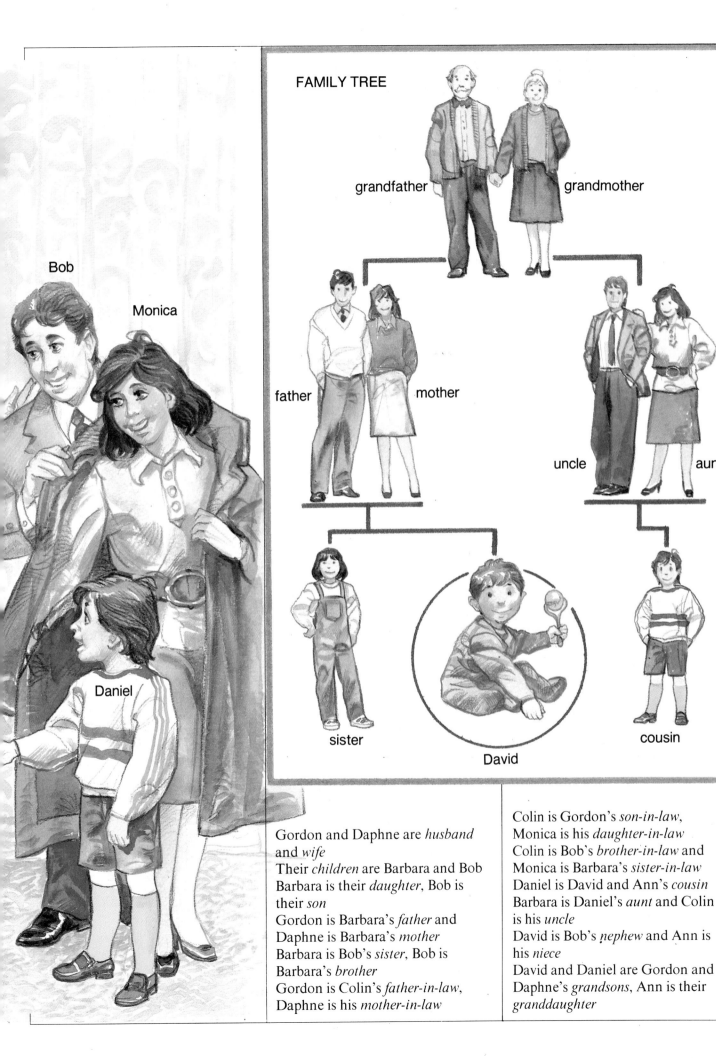

FAMILY TREE

grandfather grandmother

father mother

uncle aunt

sister

David

cousin

Bob

Monica

Daniel

Gordon and Daphne are *husband* and *wife*
Their *children* are Barbara and Bob
Barbara is their *daughter*, Bob is their *son*
Gordon is Barbara's *father* and Daphne is Barbara's *mother*
Barbara is Bob's *sister*, Bob is Barbara's *brother*
Gordon is Colin's *father-in-law*, Daphne is his *mother-in-law*

Colin is Gordon's *son-in-law*, Monica is his *daughter-in-law*
Colin is Bob's *brother-in-law* and Monica is Barbara's *sister-in-law*
Daniel is David and Ann's *cousin*
Barbara is Daniel's *aunt* and Colin is his *uncle*
David is Bob's *nephew* and Ann is his *niece*
David and Daniel are Gordon and Daphne's *grandsons*, Ann is their *granddaughter*

6 HOUSE AND GARDEN

– Where's mum?
– She's in the kitchen, cooking dinner.

– Is the bathroom free?

– Jenny, Andrew! Tidy your bedrooms, please!

– Where's dad?
– On the roof. He's fixing the aerial.

– I'm going to paint the back door on Saturday.
– Don't forget to mend the broken banisters, darling.

– The entrance hall is rather small and dark.

– We need a new carpet for the living room.

– Put the big suitcase in the attic, Andrew.

– Where's Andrew?
– He's in the garage, mending his bike.

The garden has a lawn and flower beds with some trees.
A hedge protects the garden.
A footpath leads to the gate from the front door.
The garage is attached to the house.
The gardening tools are kept in the little shed.
The wheelbarrow is full of garden rubbish.

– Meg! Help me hang the washing on the line, please!

– Father, are you going to cut the grass on Sunday?!

bush
hedge
plant
peg
washing line
rake
lawn-mower
grass
watering-can
spade
basket
tree
watering-pipe
foot path
dustbin
wheelbarrow

aerial

attic

roof

skylight

bedroom

bathroom

window

downstairs   upstairs

living room

dining room

kitchen

hall

back door

cellar

garage

7 THE KITCHEN

freezer

cupboard

fridge

mixer

jug

taps

sink

straws

squeezer

waste-bin

strainer

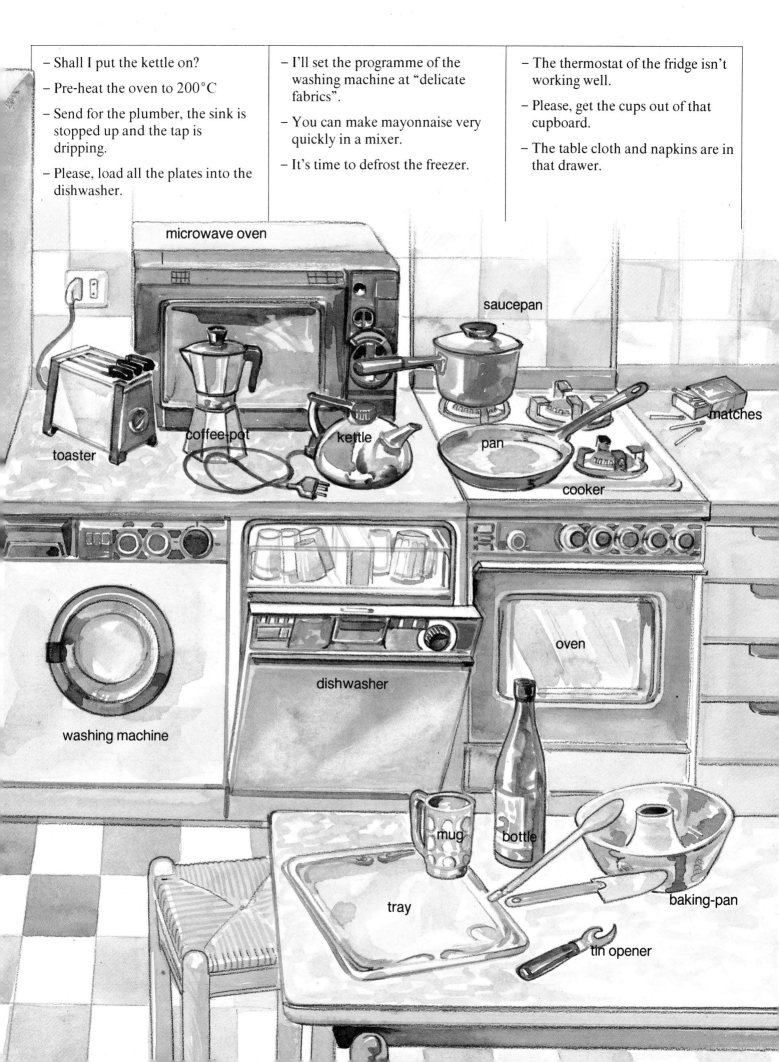

- Shall I put the kettle on?
- Pre-heat the oven to 200°C
- Send for the plumber, the sink is stopped up and the tap is dripping.
- Please, load all the plates into the dishwasher.

- I'll set the programme of the washing machine at "delicate fabrics".
- You can make mayonnaise very quickly in a mixer.
- It's time to defrost the freezer.

- The thermostat of the fridge isn't working well.
- Please, get the cups out of that cupboard.
- The table cloth and napkins are in that drawer.

microwave oven

saucepan

coffee-pot

kettle

pan

matches

toaster

cooker

oven

washing machine

dishwasher

mug

bottle

tray

baking-pan

tin opener

8 THE HALL

– Wipe your shoes on the mat, please.
  Hang your coats up on the coat rack, please.

– If your umbrella is wet, leave it outside to dry.
  If not, put it in the umbrella stand.

– Oh, dear! The lights have gone. Do you know where the fuse box is?

– May I make a phone call, please?
– Certainly, the phone is on the table in the hall.
– I'm afraid I don't know the number.
– Well, you'll find the phone book near the phone.

– Did you lock the door?
– Of course I did.
– Well, where's the key?
– Oh, dear. I must have left it in the keyhole.

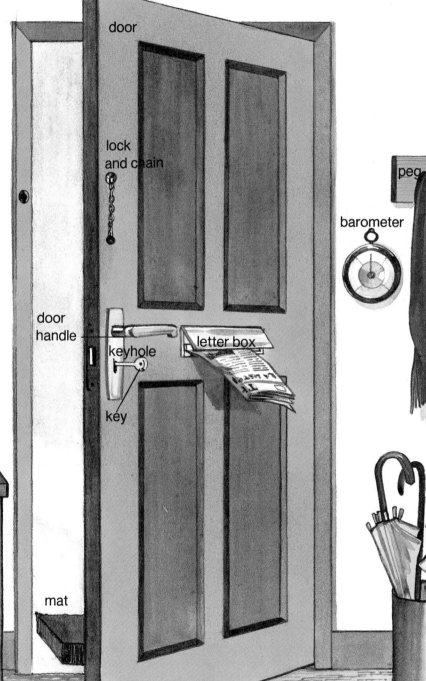

door

lock and chain

peg

barometer

switch

door handle

keyhole

letter box

key

receiver

dial

telephone book

telephone

socket

plug

mat

umbrella stand

– Where's the vacuum cleaner?
– It's with the brushes, in the cupboard under the stairs.

Children have always liked sliding down the banisters.

– I want to hang up the curtains. Would you bring me the stepladder, please?

– If you put some water in the bucket and get the mop you can wash the kitchen floor.

– Both the iron and the ironing-board are in the kitchen. Fetch them, please.

coat rack

light

STOREROOM

stepladder

fuse box

scrubbing brush

iron

ironing board

flex

handrail

broom

banister

bucket

staircase

duster

mop

stair

vacuum cleaner

9 THE WARDROBE

- Don't forget your scarf, George, it's very cold.

- I think it's going to rain, take your umbrella.

- Have you seen my gloves anywhere?
- They're in one of the pockets of your overcoat.

- But George, you can't go to the office wearing a tracksuit, you must change. You must put on your shirt, your jacket and trousers...

scarf

vest

waistcoat

jacket

overcoat

sleeve

belt

hat

pocket

umbrella

tie

trousers

collar

socks

shirt

wellington boots

gloves

– I'm going home now. Where's my coat, please?
– What colour is it?
– It's a brown fur coat.

– I always carry some make-up in my handbag.
– Oh, do you? I never use any make-up.

– Mum always wears slacks in winter, to keep her legs warm.
– Oh, does she? I don't. I wear warm wollen-tights.

– I put a clean handkerchief in my handbag every day.

fur coat

coat

dress

bra (brassière)

tights

slip (or petticoat)

blouse

handbag

skin cream

lipstick

handkerchief

shoes

beauty-case

powder compact

10 IN THE BATHROOM

– The water's too hot, turn on the cold tap, please.

– Where's the sponge?
– It's in the bath.
– I can't see it, there are so many bubbles I can't see anything.

– Stand on the bathmat Tom, the marble floor is too cold.
Put your dirty clothes in the laundry basket, please.

cabinet

razor

mirror

shaving brush

comb

brush

tube of tooth paste

tooth brush

hairdrier

hot water tap

cold water tap

plug

plug hole

nail brush

washbasin

cistern

laundry-basket

toilet paper

toilet

- Mum, you'll have to buy some toothpaste, I've just squeezed the last out of the tube.
- Pull out the plug to let the water out of the bath.
- My dad has a cold bath every morning but he rubs himself hard with the towel to warm up afterwards.
- I want to use my hairdrier, but the plug doesn't fit the socket.

shower

towel rail

bubbles

soap

scales

sponge

bath

bathmat

towel

11 THE LIVING ROOM

– That's dad's favourite armchair. He always sits in that one.

– Mum says it's bad for your eyes to sit too near the television.

– Where's the ashtray?
– It's on the mantelpiece, over the fireplace.

– Is the table laid?
– Yes, it's laid for one. If you're going to have breakfast too, bring another cup and saucer. I'll put out another table-mat.

curtain

mirror

wall

television set

mantelpiece

clock

videorecorder

fireplace

carpet

window

plant

standing lamp

frame

radio

picture

lamp

bookcase

books

newspaper

radiator

knitting needles

armchair

coffee-table

ashtray

sofa

- How many pictures are there on the wall?
- There's only one.
- How many books are there in the bookcase?
- There are too many for me to count.

A BOY'S BEDROOM

ceiling

coat hanger

cap

cardigan

pencils

book

waste paper baske[t]

pen

wardrobe

jacket

trousers

tracksuit

plimsolls (or gym-shoes)

jumper

school bag

toys

toy car

jeans

wellington-boots

- John's bed is near the window. James likes two pillows when he's reading in bed, but he throws them on the floor before going to sleep.

- I didn't hear the alarm clock this morning, so I was late for school.

- When my bedroom gets untidy I pick up all my clothes and toys and throw them into the wardrobe.
  It's like magic:when I close the door, my room is tidy!

- I have a desk in my bedroom and I usually study there.

- How many blankets do you have on your bed?
- Three in winter but only one in summer.

radiator

pyjamas

blanket

pillowcase

T-shirt

vest

pants

sheet

shirt

bed

slippers

socks

rug

A GIRL'S BEDROOM

– Where's my anorak, mum?
– It's hanging up in the wardrobe.

– If you don't fasten your buckle, Jane, you'll lose your belt.
– All right mum, but first I'll fasten my sandals.

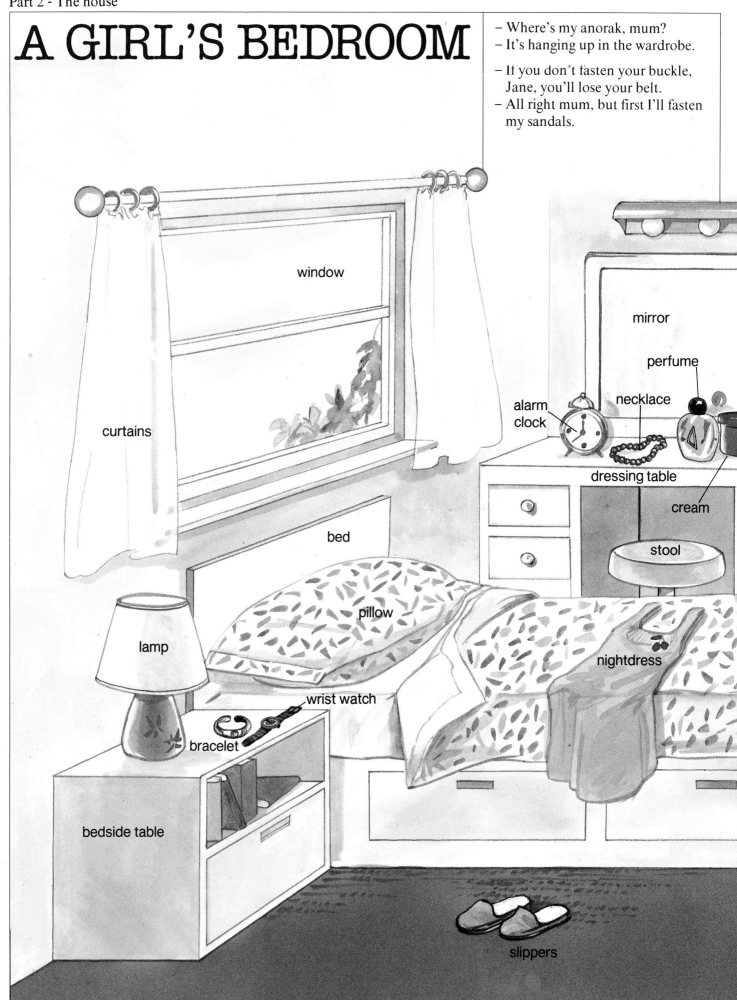

window

mirror

perfume

necklace

alarm clock

curtains

dressing table

cream

bed

stool

pillow

lamp

nightdress

wrist watch

bracelet

bedside table

slippers

– Helen is wearing two gold bracelets and a gold wrist watch. She must be very rich.

– Why does Janet always wear a shawl when she's sitting up in bed?
– To keep her shoulders warm dear.

– Does she wear slippers in bed, too?
– No, she doesn't, but she sometimes wears bedsocks.

wardrobe

ribbon

scarf

hat

belt

blouse

buckle

hair brush

skirt

jumper

anorak

sandals

tights

rocking-chair

drawer

A BUILDING SITE

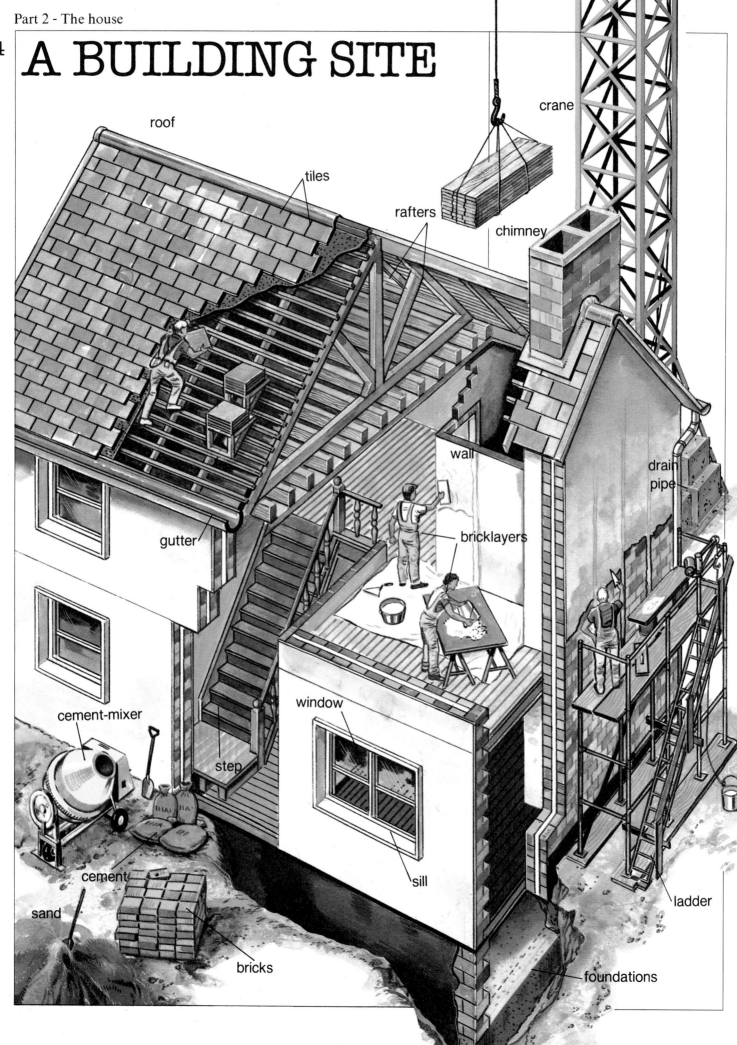

roof

tiles

crane

rafters

chimney

wall

drain pipe

gutter

bricklayers

cement-mixer

window

step

sill

cement

ladder

sand

bricks

foundations

The men are building a new house.
They climb a ladder to get up on
the roof.
They put red tiles on the roof.
The crane lifts the heavy rafters and
places them in the right position.
The foundations are strong: the
house will not fall down.
Cement holds the bricks together.
Gutters and drain-pipes carry away
the rain water.
The very small house is a
bungalow. It has only one floor.

– I never use a lift. I live in a
  bungalow.

– I live in a period house. It was
  built in the sixteenth century.

– We have rented a cottage in the
  country for the summer.

– One of those terraced houses
  opposite us is for sale.

– Sky-scrapers can be very high, but
  they never touch the sky.

– Once upon a time there was a
  good king who lived in a castle...

HOUSES

sky-scraper

balcony

cottage
a timber house

balcony

front door

castle

bungalow

shutter

lawn

gate

block of flats

front door

foot path

detached house

terraced houses

15 BREAKFAST

– This isn't tea, it's hot water!

– Good heavens! That means I forgot to put the tea in.

– Mmmm. I smell sausages! I love crisp sausages first thing in the morning.

– Help yourself to toast. Butter it yourself, Billy.

– May I have some more sugar with my cornflakes please, mum?

– A cup of black coffee will soon wake you up!

cocoa

marmalade

cheese

fruit juice

bread

toast

glass

honey

milk

sugar

fork

plate

croissant

salami

sausages

biscuits

tea

salt

pepper

butter

coffee

cup

fried eggs and bacon

cornflakes

.spoon

porridge

mug

bowl

yoghurt

knife

jam

napkin

16

LUNCH

– Let's try this self-service. It looks clean.

– Take your tray and don't forget the cutlery.

– I'm going to have meat pie, salad and a beer.
– I'm not hungry, I'll just have a cup of tea.
– I want fish and chips, hamburgers and sausages. And a coke.
– Are you all together?
  Then it's £ 6.10 altogether.

PRICE LIST

serviettes

cutlery

trays

fish

meat pie

roast chicken

green beans

chips

salad

cheese

apple pie

glass

oil

vinegar

pepper

salt

hamburgers

sausages

steak

tomatoes

bread

cashier

crème caramel

fruit salad

mineral water

wine

coke

cash desk

beer

DINNER

17

– What's for dinner? I'm as hungry as a horse.

– This roast-beef is delicious.
– You haven't tried the chicken.

– Eat up all your sprouts. Vegetables are good for you.
– May I have two sweets instead of vegetables, please, mum?

"I scream, you scream... We all scream for ice-cream".!

fork

beer

ladle

knife

vegetable soup

spoon

tureen

roast chicken

roast beef

water

half chicken

meat dish

lamb chops

table cloth

basket of fruits

cider

apple

orange

banana

pear

grapes

apple pie

ice cream

wine

glass

plate

napkin

cheese
and biscuits

sprouts

roast potatoes

18 CHRISTMAS

- Father Christmas has a lot of presents in his sack.

- Holly is used to decorate houses at Christmas.

- I received a lot of Christmas cards this year and I hung them up in my bedroom.

- I like decorating the Christmas tree. Mother says candles are dangerous so I use coloured lights.

- We put a lighted Christmas candle at the window on Christmas Eve.

Christmas tree

snowman

holly

Christmas card

Merry Christmas

Christmas cake

presents

sack

doll

December

24 - Christmas Eve

25 - Christmas Day

26 - Boxing Day

toy car

electric train

teddy bear

crib

Father Christmas

NEW YEAR - EASTER

- On the last day of the year, called New Year's Eve, most people go to parties. When the clock strikes twelve, they all exchange greetings and kisses.
  Then they make a big circle and sing "Auld lang syne".

- The first person to enter the house on New Year's Day must be a dark haired man. He is called "the first foot".

- Easter eggs are usually made of chocolate.

- Sometimes we colour eggs on Easter Sunday by boiling them with different things in water. Then we eat them.

- Once, in England, there was the tradition of the Easter bonnet, the pretty new hat to wear to church on Easter Sunday. Now the children have new clothes to wear on Easter Sunday.

toast

plum pudding

New Year's Eve
31 DECEMBER
New Year's Day
JANUARY

calendar

olive branches

bell

chocolate Bunny

Happy Easter

card

chick

Easter egg

eggs

20 BIRTHDAY PARTY

– It's John's birthday today.
– Oh, how old is he?
– He's seven.

– Can you blow out all the candles together?

– Did you get a lot of presents for your birthday?

– It's Elizabeth's birthday next week. I must remember to send her a card.

– Let's pull a cracker...

garlands

lollypops

birthday card

marshmallows

candies

gifts

peanuts

orange squash

Happy birthday to you,
Happy birthday to you,
Happy birthday dear Peter
Happy birthday to you!

cracker

paper hat

candles

straw

birthday cake

coca-cola

chocolates

highchair

popcorn

21 CARNIVAL

- During carnival time children and grown-ups often wear fancy dress.
- People wear masks so as not to be recognized.
- I went to a fancy dress party dressed as a clown.
- In England people throw confetti on the bride and bridegroom at weddings. In Italy they throw confetti at everyone during carnival time.
- Hallowe'en is the evening before All Saints' Day. "Hallow" means 'holy'.
- People say that witches fly through the air on their broomsticks at Hallowe'en.

bells

jester

ballerina

Punchinello (or Punch)

mask

tutu (or ballet skirt)

cowboy

Columbine

witch

false nose

Harlequin

clown

gun

wizard

domino

moustache

festoon

paper lantern

devil

cook

gipsy girl

streamer

odalisque
(or bayadère)

veil

mandarin

fan

dame

pirate

blindfold

Pierrot

confetti

turnip lantern

BARALDI

THE CLASSROOM

- Miss Simpson is using the chalk.
- Give me a ruler, please. I want to draw a line.
- All right. Do you want a compass as well?

map

calendar

MAY

duster

text book

exercise-book

globe

school bag

wastepaper bin

paint brushes

- Oh, I'm sorry! I've spilt the paint on your exercise book.
- Never mind! I've spilt some glue on your schoolbag.

- What day is tomorrow?
- I don't know. Look at the calendar.

- Don't use your calculator, Dick. Use your head!
- May I use the computer, Miss Simpson?
- Yes, of course. But don't write yet. Wait until I put the disk in!

blackboard

timetable

TIMETABLE FOR TUESDAYS

9.00 assembly	11.55 lunch and free time
9.20 english	13.05 careers
9.55 maths	14.20 religious education
10.30 break	14.55 chemistry
10.45 french	15.30 woodwork club
11.20 music (guitar)	17.00 home

teacher

chalk

calculator

poster

palette

a pair of compasses

schoolgirl

set-square

glue

paints

thumbtacks

pencil

rubber

ruler

a pair of scissors

pen

NUMBERS

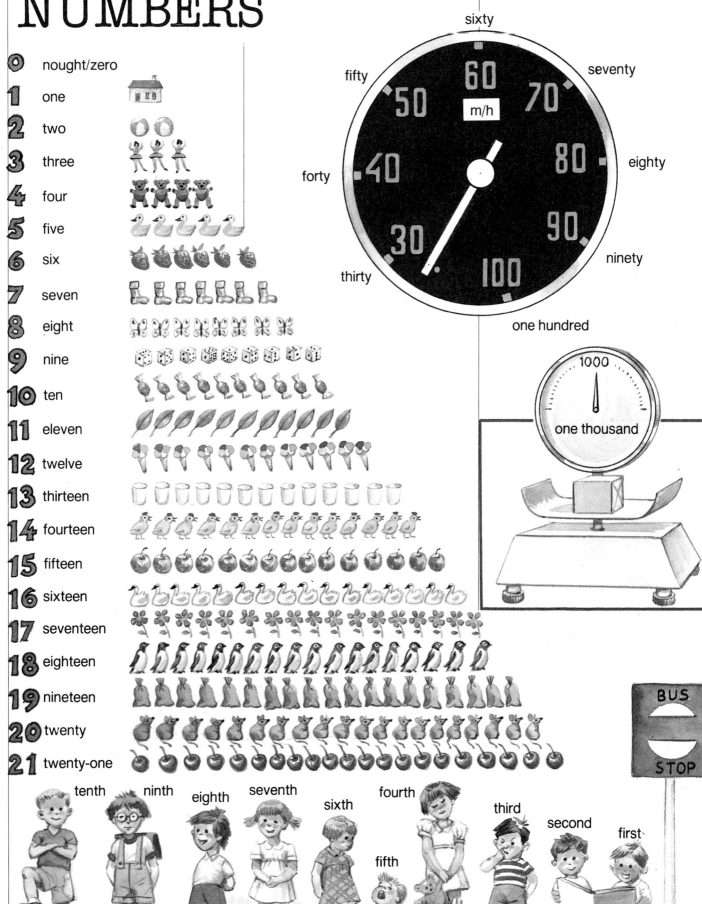

23

0	nought/zero
1	one
2	two
3	three
4	four
5	five
6	six
7	seven
8	eight
9	nine
10	ten
11	eleven
12	twelve
13	thirteen
14	fourteen
15	fifteen
16	sixteen
17	seventeen
18	eighteen
19	nineteen
20	twenty
21	twenty-one

sixty
fifty
seventy
forty
eighty
thirty
ninety
one hundred

m/h

one thousand

BUS STOP

tenth ninth eighth seventh sixth fourth third second first fifth

MATHS

ARITHMETIC, CALCULATION BY NUMBERS

add   Three *plus* three equals six.

subtract   Six *minus* three equals three.

multiply   Three *times* four equals twelve.   Three *multiplied by* four equals twelve.

divide   Twelve *divided by* four equals three.

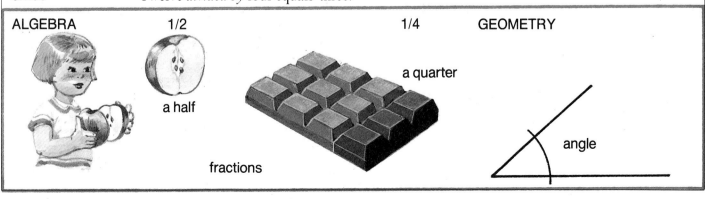

ALGEBRA   1/2   1/4   GEOMETRY

a quarter

a half

angle

fractions

25 SHAPES AND LINES

LINES

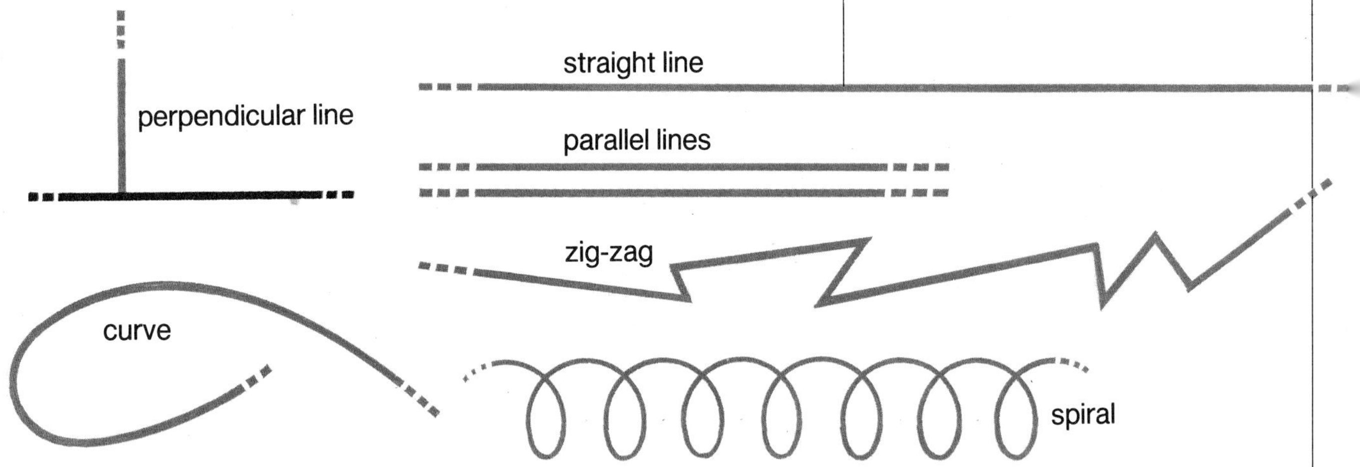

perpendicular line

straight line

parallel lines

zig-zag

curve

spiral

PLANE FIGURES

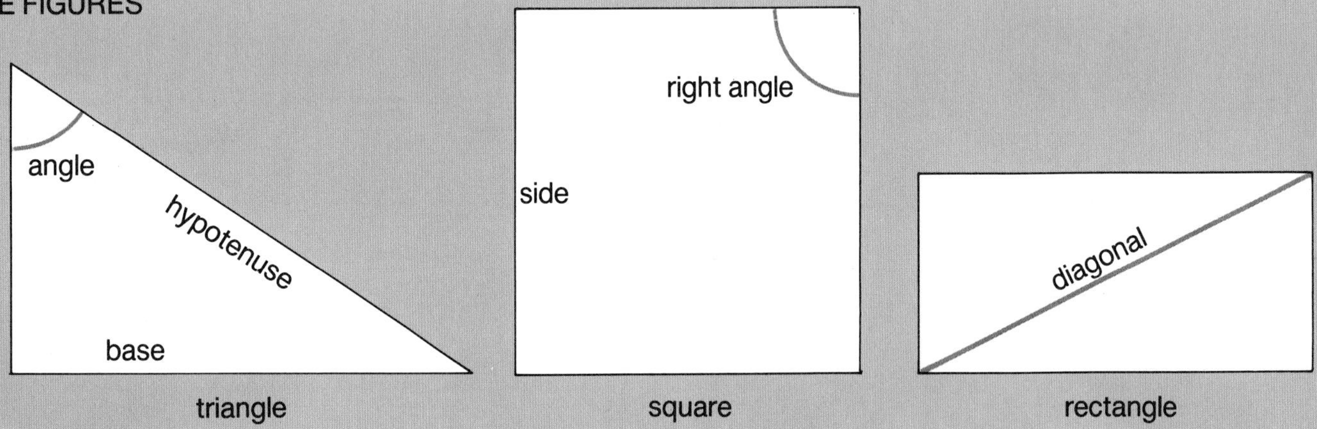

angle
hypotenuse
base

triangle

right angle
side

square

diagonal

rectangle

SOLID FIGURES

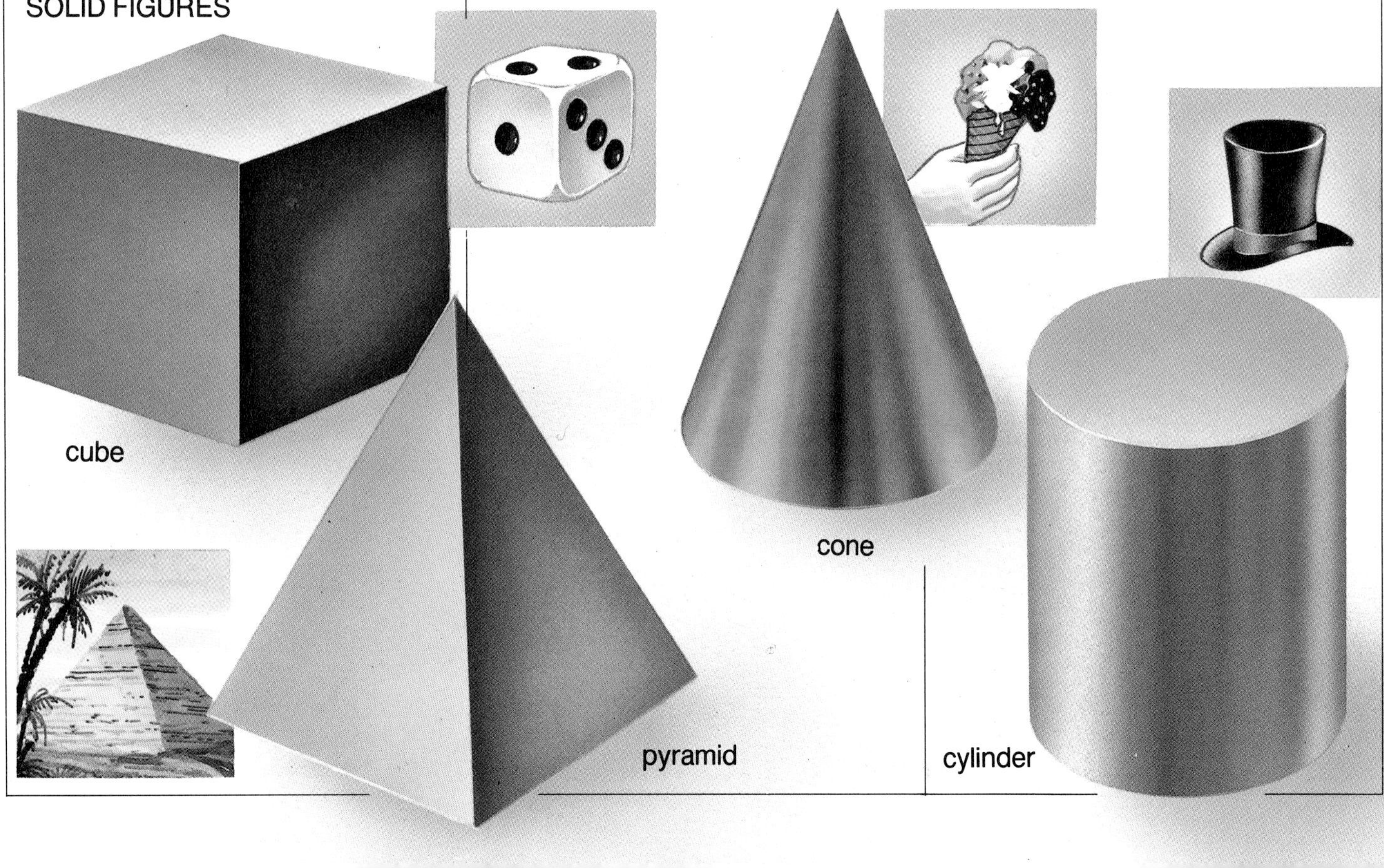

cube

pyramid

cone

cylinder

If two halves make a whole and four quarters make a whole, the two quarters must make a half.

– Why are parallel lines unsociable?
– I don't know. Why are parallel lines unsociable?
– Because they never meet!

If you ask a drunk man to walk on a straight line he will probably go zig-zag.

– Can you give me the width and height of your television set?
– I'm afraid I don't know.
– Well, just measure from the top to bottom, that's the height; then measure from one side to another, that's the width.

A diameter is a line that divides a circle in two halves.

– I like cones when they are upside-down and filled with ice-cream!

The famous pyramids in Eygpt are square because they are built on square bases.

– How many sides does a triangle have?
– That's easy. It has three sides.

– Who discovered the theorem about a right-angled triangle?
– It was a Greek philosopher, Pythagoras:
"The square on the hypotenuse of a right-angled triangle is equal in area to the sum of the squares on the other two sides".

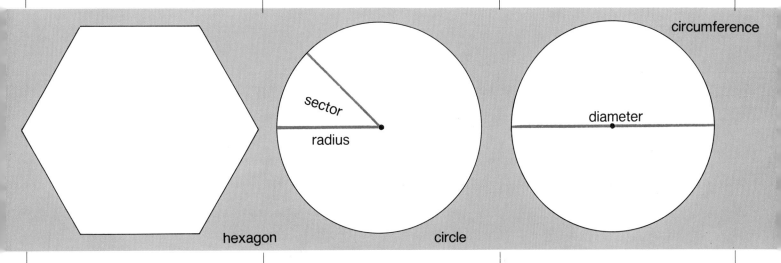

hexagon

sector
radius

circle

circumference
diameter

sphere

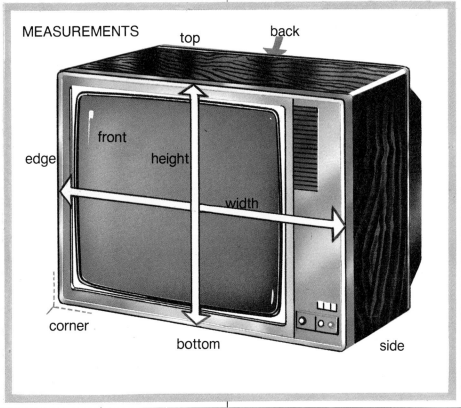

MEASUREMENTS

back
top
front
edge
height
width
corner
bottom
side

COLOURS

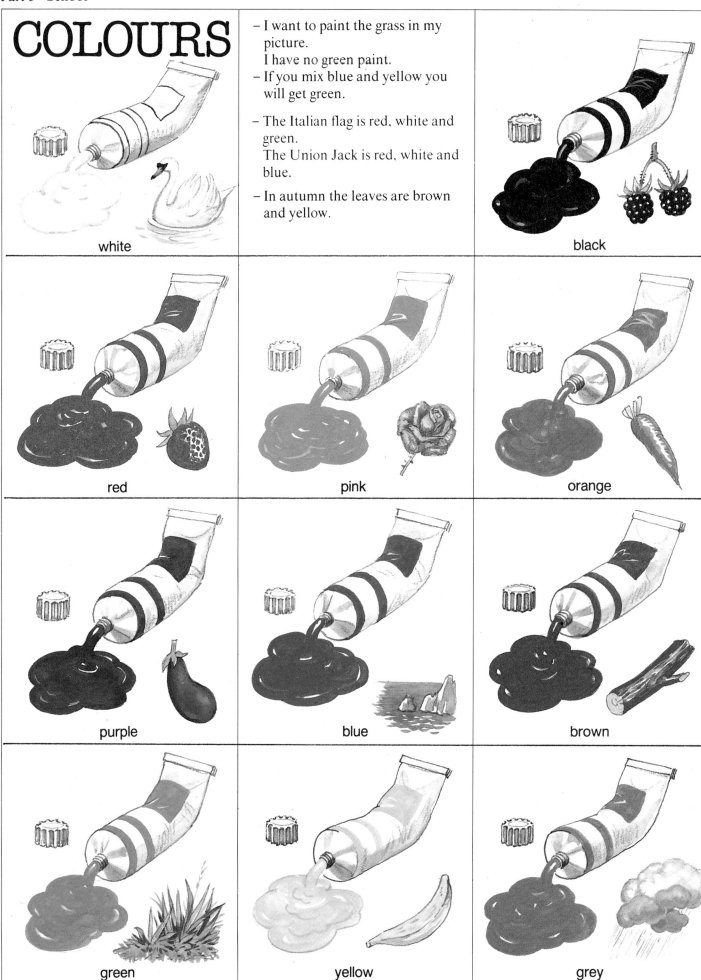

26

white

– I want to paint the grass in my picture.
  I have no green paint.
– If you mix blue and yellow you will get green.

– The Italian flag is red, white and green.
  The Union Jack is red, white and blue.

– In autumn the leaves are brown and yellow.

black

red

pink

orange

purple

blue

brown

green

yellow

grey

blackboard

– Put on your earphones.
Switch on your tape recorder.
Listen carefully and repeat.
If you want to call the teacher,
press the white button.
Straighten your earphones,
they're crooked.
When the tape is finished, press
the rewind button.

teacher

earphones

control buttons

console

pupil

microphone

headset

cassette recorder

translation

volume control

dictionary

pencil

O.H.P. (Overhead projector)

THE SCIENCE LABORATORY

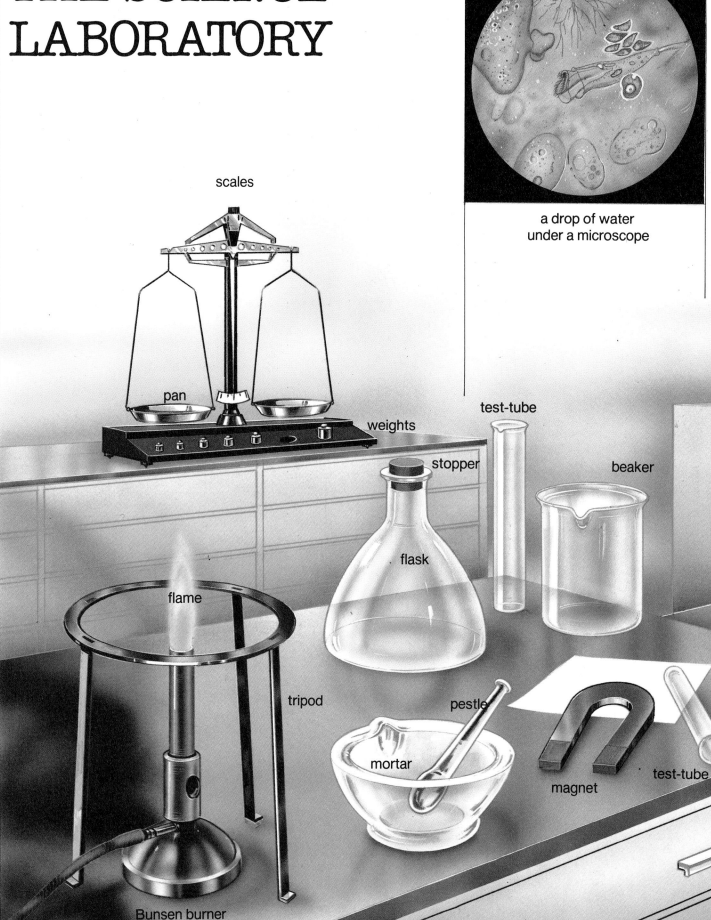

a drop of water
under a microscope

scales

pan

weights

stopper

test-tube

beaker

flask

flame

tripod

pestle

mortar

magnet

test-tube

Bunsen burner

A Bunsen burner provides heat for chemical experiments.

- Have you ever seen a drop of water under a microscope?

- The test-tube was cracked, that's why it exploded when I held it over the flame.

- Take the stopper out of the flask, before trying to pour the liquid.

- Dissolve the salt crystals in water.

- I've got the weights but I can't find the scales.

- One day we'll blow up the lab during chemistry class...

still

condenser

flame

ocular

lens

dropper

slides

mirror

microscope

crystals

GYMNASTICS

punch ball

punch bag

horse

mat

wall bars

rope

trampoline

hoop

beam

weight-lifting

referee

glove

boxer

sparring partner

ropes

ring

rings

parallel bars

window ladder

clubs

- Wall bars are good for developing your shoulder muscles.

- Have you seen John climbing the rope?
- No, why?
- He goes up as quick as lightening. He climbs it like a fireman.

backboard

ball

basket

players

judoka

coloured belt

kimono

- Children play with hoops and skipping ropes, but you will find them in a gym as well.

- Don't worry if you fall, the mattress is very soft.

- That's a vaulting horse, you must vault it, not ride it.

- Acrobats often use a trampoline or springboard when they do spectacular sommersaults.

TRAFFIC

– Taxi! Taxi!
– Yes, madam?
– Please take me to the airport quickly!

Pedestrians cross the road when the traffic lights are green.

The pillar box is outside the post office.

– Mum, what's the policeman doing in the middle of the road?
– He's on point duty. He's directing the traffic.

– I live at number 2, Atholl Crescent.
– Why is it called "crescent"?
– Because of its shape. It's like a half moon.

– Where's the newsagent's, please?
– It's the shop on the right-hand corner of this street.

– I toured Spain by coach, it was a very comfortable journey.

– When dad comes home there's always a lot of traffic. When I come home there are never any buses.

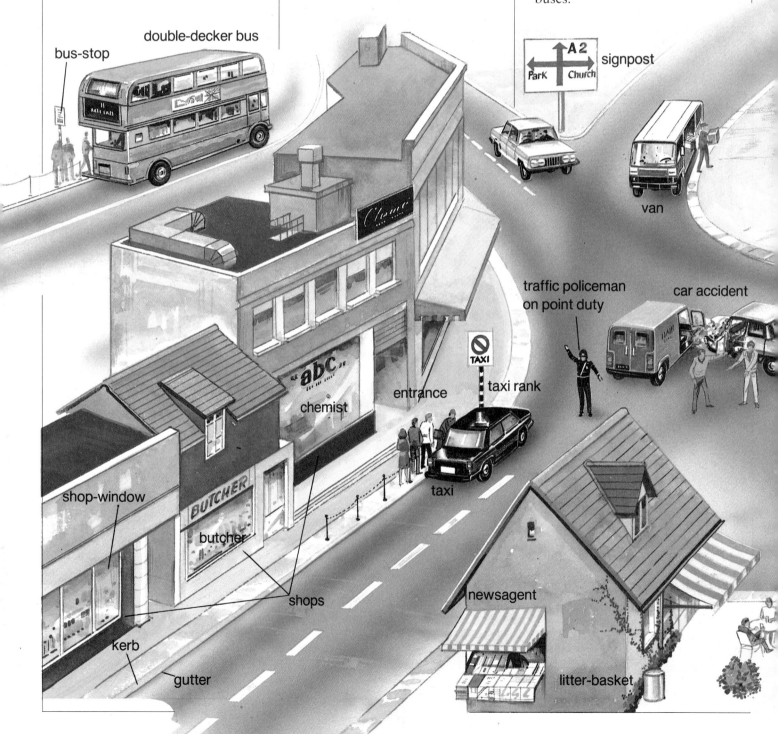

bus-stop

double-decker bus

A 2
Park   Church
signpost

van

traffic policeman on point duty

car accident

entrance   taxi rank

chemist

shop-window

butcher

taxi

shops

newsagent

kerb

gutter

litter-basket

department store

hotel

post office

Post Office

pillar box

car

POLICE

lorry

square

lamp-post

coach

traffic-lights

bike

motorbike

telephone box
(or call-box)

pedestrians

pedestrian crossing

drain

31 A SUPERMARKET

Customers must take a trolley when they enter the supermarket.
When they have finished shopping, they have to queue at the cash-desk to pay.

– Where can I find tinned foods, please?
– They're on the other side of this shelf.
– Thank you.

– Do you want fresh fish or frozen fish?
– Frozen fish and vegetables, please.
– Well, you'll find them in the frozen foods section, over there on your right.

– Here's your change and I've put your receipt in the paper bag with your groceries.

detergents
shelf
drinks
groceries
fruit
tinned foods
cash-register
cashier
receipt
cash desk
vegetables
customer
purse
trolley

manager

forklift

stocks of tea and coffee

pallet

supply of fruits and vegetables

chickens, roasting on the spit

cheese

milk

meat

eggs

frozen foods

freezer

fish

basket

bread

ABOUT THE MARKET

– Mum, are you making marmalade
or jam?
– Look, Sara, I'm using oranges and
lemons, so I'm making
marmalade.

– Dad, can we make wine with our
apples?
– No, we can't. Wine comes from
grapes.

pineapples

cherries

lemons

pears

figs

bananas

apples

watermelons

oranges

melons

strawberries

dates

grapes

peaches

– I'd like a big mixed salad for lunch.
– Let's go to the market, then. We'll buy some lettuce, some tomatoes and some carrots.
– What about some peppers?
– Oh, yes, and some cucumbers, too.

We get oil from olives.

Mushrooms grow very quickly.

Garlic adds flavour to food.

Popeye always eats spinach.

Never throw a banana skin on the street.

Strawberries are red.

Dates grow on tall palm trees.

garlic
olives
onions

courgettes
Brussels sprouts
aubergines
tomatoes

carrots
peas
beans
lettuce

cabbage
peppers
spinach
cucumbers

potatoes
mushrooms
string-beans

A BAKER'S SHOP

- Today's Saturday, let's buy a cake.
- Yes, let's. Which one shall we buy?
- Let's ask how much that chocolate cream cake costs.

- May I have three rolls, please, and a small French loaf?

- I'd like some biscuits, please.
- Chocolate biscuits or plain biscuits?
- Both, please, and a slice of fruit flan.

A BUTCHER'S SHOP

salami

sausages

scales

shop assistant

– I want some bacon and sausages, please.
It's for Sunday morning breakfast.

– If you want to make a meat sauce for your spaghetti you must buy some minced meat.

– I'd like two slices of Bolognese sausage, please.

ham

Bolognese sausage

cutlet

tinned meat

Vienna sausage

pork   veal   rabbit

duck

chop

joints

chicken   bacon   pâté

beef

minced meat

fillet

steak

pre-packed joints

deep freezer

35 A GROCER'S SHOP

- I want a bottle of whisky, please.
- Irish or Scotch?
- What's the difference between the two?
- Irish whiskey is made in Ireland and is spelt with an "e", Scotch whisky is made in Scotland.

- May I have a glass of brandy, please?

- I'm sorry, I can't sell you a *glass* of brandy. I sell brandy by the bottle.

- Which is heavier, a pound of tea or a pound of coffee?
- I've heard that one before. They both weigh the same, of course!

bottled wine

whisky

oil

spaghetti

peaches in sirup

tinned fruit

macaroni

peeled tomatoes

fruit juice

tinned vegetables

chick-peas

(green peas

Apple

A DEPARTMENT STORE

FIRST FLOOR

FABRIC DEPARTMENT

rolls of cloth

lift

customers

shop assistant
(or sales girl)

jewels

JEWELLERY DEPARTMENT

1 - LADIES' WEAR
2 - MEN'S WEAR
3 - HOUSEHOLD
     ARTICLES
4 - FURNISHINGS
5 - TOYS AND
     SPORTS WEAR
6 - BAR

dummy

coat hanger

jacket

changing
booth

mirror

- May I try one of those blouses hanging on the clothes rack over there?
- They're all outsize. They would be too big for you.
- Let's ask the shop assistant where the glove counter is.

shoes

escalator

2°FLOOR

shawl

stockings

clothes rack

shelves

dresses

blouse

cashier

gloves

cash register

counter

LADIES' WEAR DEPARTMENT

- My granny doesn't like escalators, she always wants to use the lift.
- If you want to buy a pair of tights you must look for the hosiery department.
- Please wait for your receipt, madam!

37 TRAVEL BY ROAD

England has an intricate network of *roads*.

London has an intricate network of *streets*.

– What's the difference between a street and an avenue?

– When an avenue is a street, there should be trees on either side.

There are no traffic lights at a roundabout.

– How many lanes of traffic are there on a motorway?

spur

grove

road markings

container lorry

transporter

moped   fly-over

underpass

caravan

TOWERS
WYCOMBE   traffic
signs

coach

trailer

inside lane

three-wheeler

child's scooter

– It depends. There are always at least two.

– Excuse me. Can you tell me the way to Wycombe?

– Certainly. Do you see the motorway flyover, over there? Well, drive straight on; after the flyover you'll see the sign to Wycombe.

– Traffic on the motorway was diverted this morning. A petrol tanker overturned. There was petrol everywhere.

When people have a lot of luggage, they put it in a trailer.

– Uncle Jimmy is going to buy a sports car. Why don't we buy a sports car, mum?

– Because there are six of us. We need a large car. We use it to tow our caravan, too!

ring road

roundabout

avenue

road

tanker

three-way tipper

articulated lorry

street

telephone

motorway

terrace

sports car

ambulance

guardrail

emergency lane

outside lane

38 TRAFFIC SIGNS

When pedestrians don't use the pedestrian crossings they are called "jaywalkers".

– There must be a school near here, look at that sign indicating children.
Slow down, George, if there's any traffic coming from the left you must give way.
You mustn't blow your horn here, that "H" stands for hospital.
It's a one-way street, so we'll have to go round to the other end, if we want to drive in.
You can't park here. That's a "no waiting" sign!

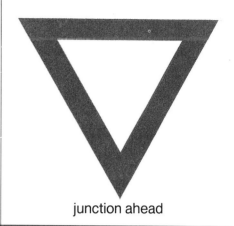

junction ahead

two-way traffic

children

cross roads

bend to the right

pedestrian crossing

traffic signals

road works

level crossing without barrier ahead

other danger

A CAR

– Shall we put the suitcases in the boot?
– Yes let's.

– Fasten your safety belts, children. Are you all ready? Let's go.

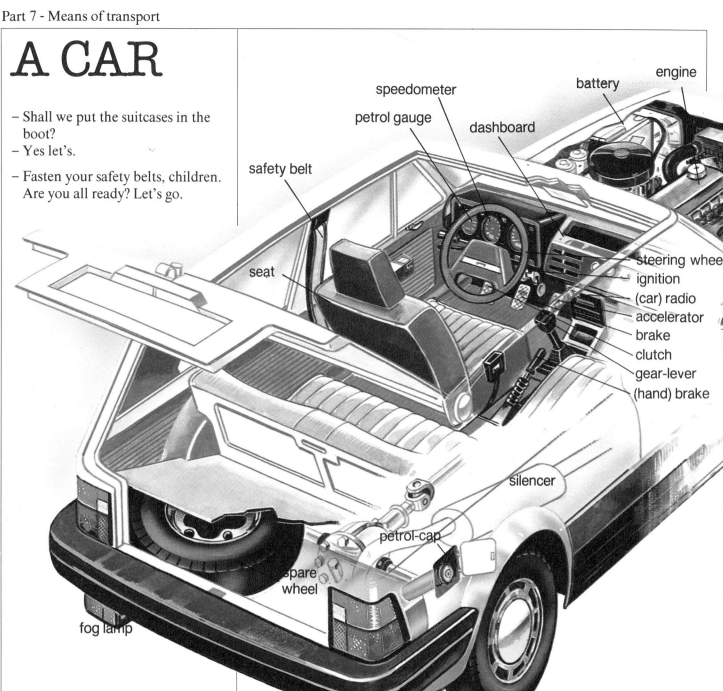

speedometer

petrol gauge

safety belt

dashboard

battery

engine

safety belt

seat

steering wheel

ignition

(car) radio

accelerator

brake

clutch

gear-lever

(hand) brake

silencer

petrol-cap

spare wheel

fog lamp

exhaust-pipe

– When you want to go fast you press the accelerator.
Drivers use the windscreen wipers when it rains.
When you drive in the dark you must turn on your lights. The headlights are at the front and the rearlights are at the back.
When you overtake another car, you should blow your horn.

– Oh! Why did you brake so suddenly, daddy?
– Because a man crossed the road in front of the car.

– Why didn't he see you?
– Because he didn't look right before crossing.
Oh, dear. Look at the petrol gauge.
There's no petrol in the tank.

– Twenty litres of petrol please, and put some water in the radiator. Here are the keys.
– Anythings else, sir?
– Oh, will you check the pressure of the tyres, too?
– Yes, sir.

PETROL STATION

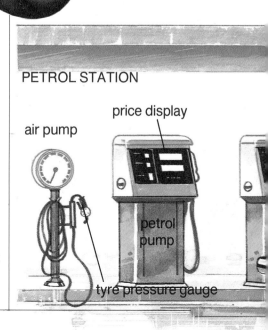

air pump

price display

petrol pump

tyre pressure gauge

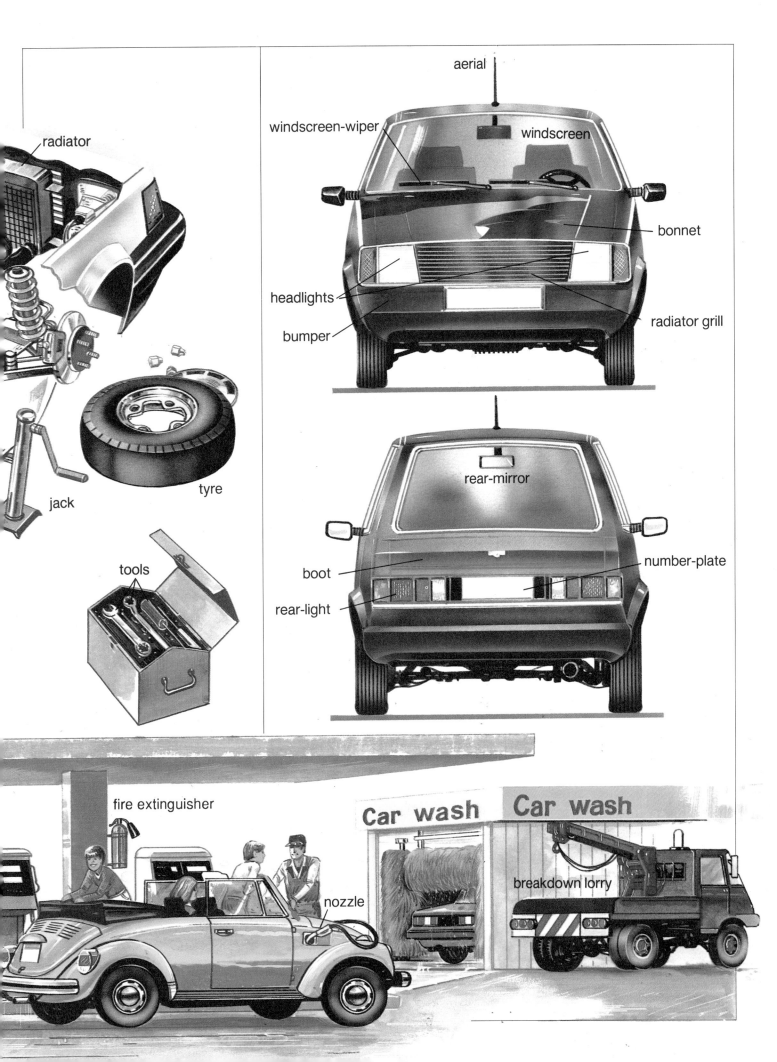

radiator

jack

tyre

tools

aerial

windscreen-wiper

windscreen

bonnet

headlights

bumper

radiator grill

rear-mirror

boot

number-plate

rear-light

fire extinguisher

nozzle

Car wash

Car wash

breakdown lorry

40 A MOTORBIKE

– Double-disk brakes are the safest. Mind your feet don't slip off the footrests.
– Oh, it's been raining, the saddle is all wet and the roads will be slippery...

– Look, your motorbike has an indicator just like a car.

– Take me for a ride, Johnny.
– Sorry, I can't. I promised my father I wouldn't take anyone on the pillion.

– My chinstrap it to long. What shall I do?
– Shorten it!

– I chain my helmet to my motorbike. What do you do with yours?
– That's a good idea. I always carry mine around with me - it's a nuisance.

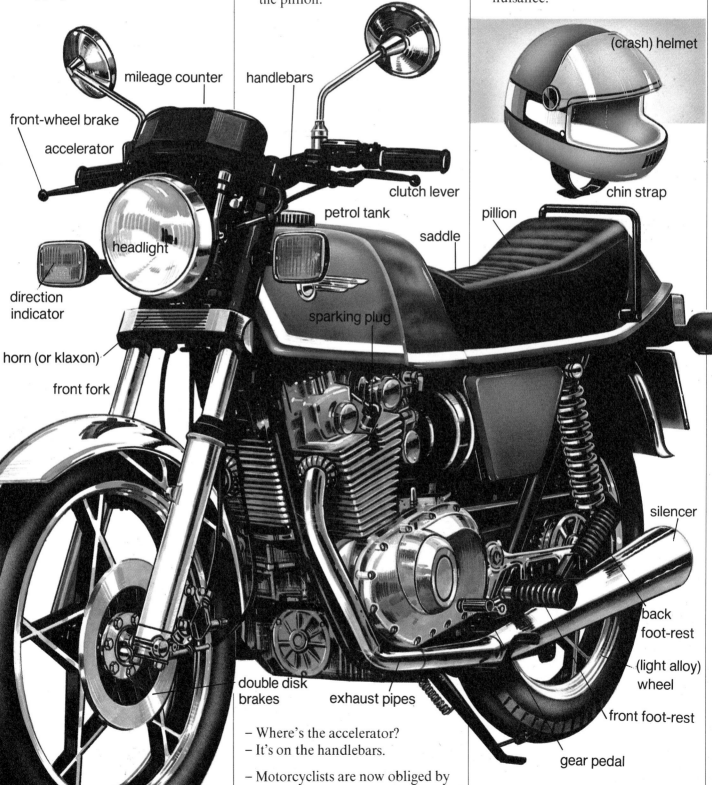

mileage counter

front-wheel brake

accelerator

handlebars

(crash) helmet

chin strap

clutch lever

petrol tank

pillion

saddle

headlight

direction indicator

sparking plug

horn (or klaxon)

front fork

silencer

back foot-rest

(light alloy) wheel

double disk brakes

exhaust pipes

front foot-rest

gear pedal

– Where's the accelerator?
– It's on the handlebars.

– Motorcyclists are now obliged by law to wear crash helmets.

lock

saddle bags

– Where's the pump? My front tyre is flat.

– Come on, let's go. I'll take you on *my* bike.
– But there are three of us.
– You'll sit on the handlebars, Tom can sit on the crossbar, I'll sit on the saddle and pedal furiously.

– My mac is very dirty because there's no mudguard on my bicycle.

– People sometimes forget that a reflector is just as important as a lamp when cycling in the dark.

saddle

bell

grip

handlebars

tool bag

brake

mudguard

reflector

dynamo

crossbar

(rear) lamp

lamp

pump

hub

spokes

chain

pedal

tyres

42 | TRAVEL BY TRAIN

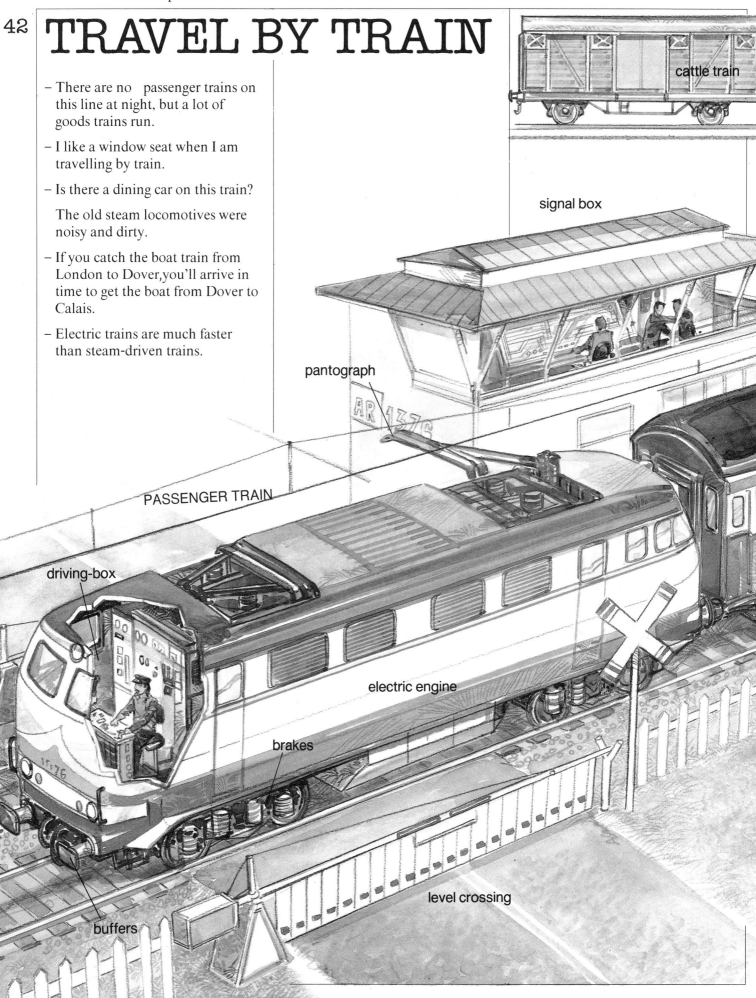

- There are no passenger trains on this line at night, but a lot of goods trains run.

- I like a window seat when I am travelling by train.

- Is there a dining car on this train?

  The old steam locomotives were noisy and dirty.

- If you catch the boat train from London to Dover, you'll arrive in time to get the boat from Dover to Calais.

- Electric trains are much faster than steam-driven trains.

cattle train

signal box

pantograph

PASSENGER TRAIN

driving-box

electric engine

brakes

level crossing

buffers

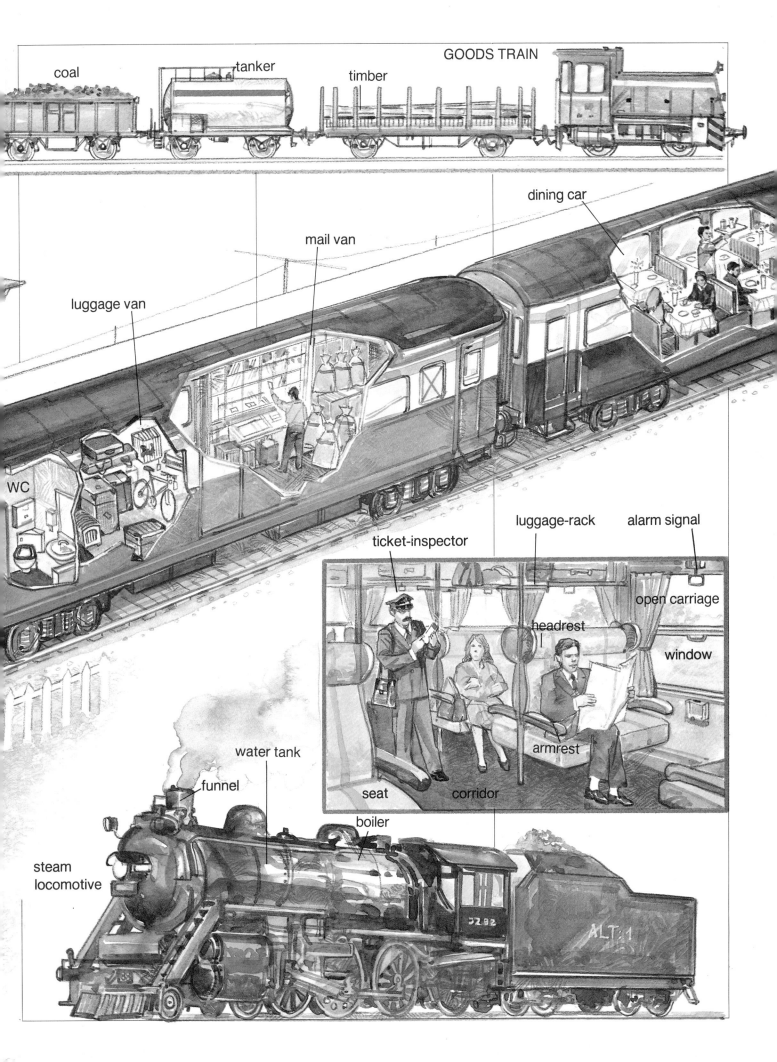

GOODS TRAIN

coal

tanker

timber

dining car

mail van

luggage van

WC

ticket-inspector

luggage-rack

alarm signal

open carriage

headrest

window

armrest

seat

corridor

water tank

funnel

boiler

steam locomotive

THE STATION

43

station clock

arrivals and departures board

"The 3.30 train from Manchester is arriving at platform number 2."

– Tickets, please.
– Here's my ticket.
– Thank you.

– Let's take a taxi.
– All right. Let's look for the taxi rank. There's always one at a station.

– Would you like to do a coach tour of the Lake District?
– That would be lovely dear.

waiting-room

ticket-office

loudspeaker

ticket

platform number

ticket-collector

bookstall

railway-line

porter

luggage

platform

escalators

underground station

– Let's look at the timetable. Oh dear, what a pity!
– What's wrong?
– We've just missed the last train to Edinburgh.

– My daddy's an engine driver. He drives trains.

– Look, the guard is waving his flag.
– Then the train will leave now.

– That's funny. There's no one in the waiting room.
– Well, the last train has just left!

left-luggage office

coach

bus

taxi

barrier

bench

passengers

train

flag

guard

electric trolley

driver

engine

carriage

AIRPLANE AND HELICOPTER

A jet aeroplane is pushed by a jet engine.
A helicopter is very noisy and makes a lot of dust fly when it lands.

air hostess

passengers

AIRCRAFT IN LOADING POSITION

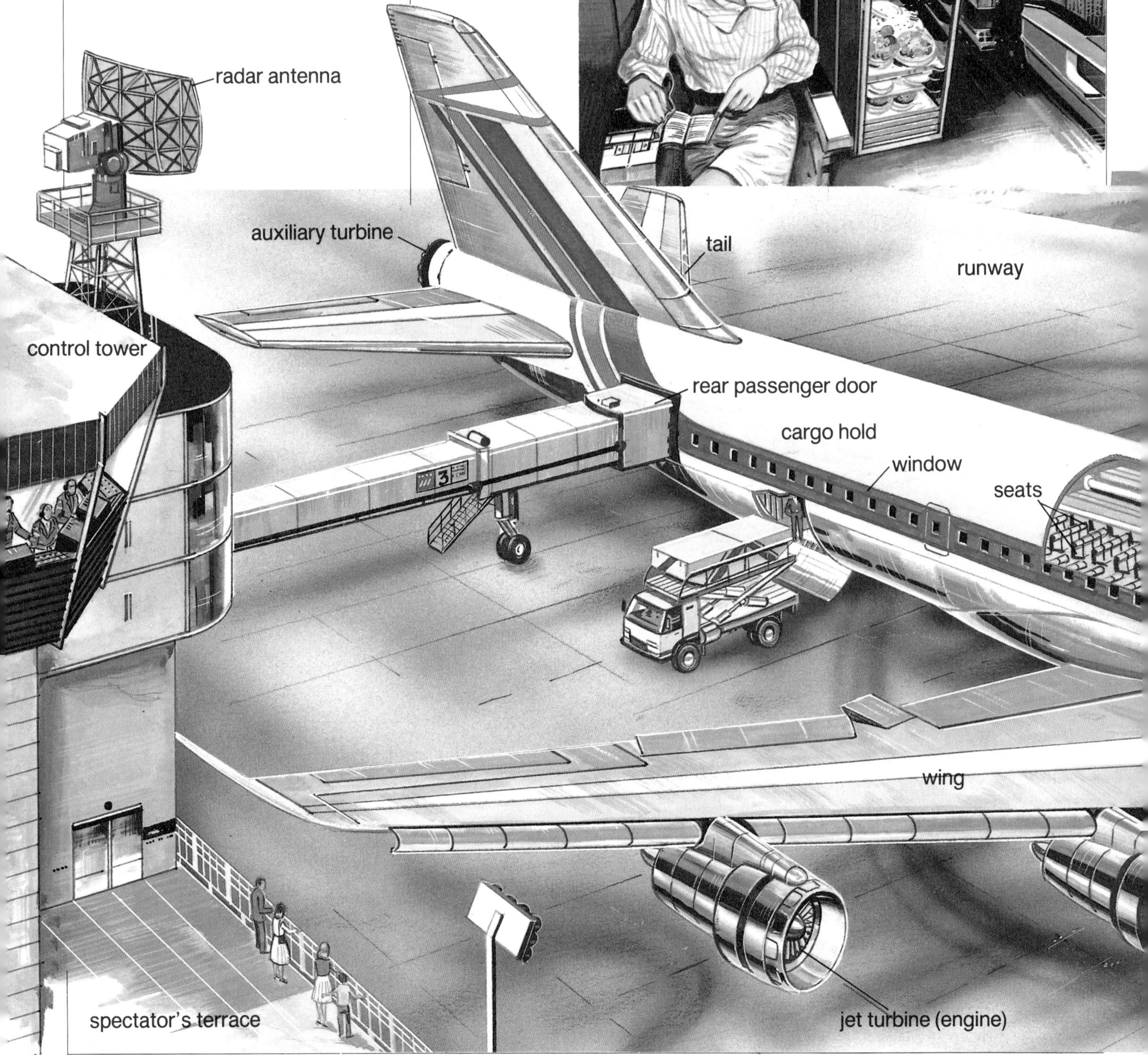

radar antenna

auxiliary turbine

tail

runway

control tower

rear passenger door

cargo hold

window

seats

wing

spectator's terrace

jet turbine (engine)

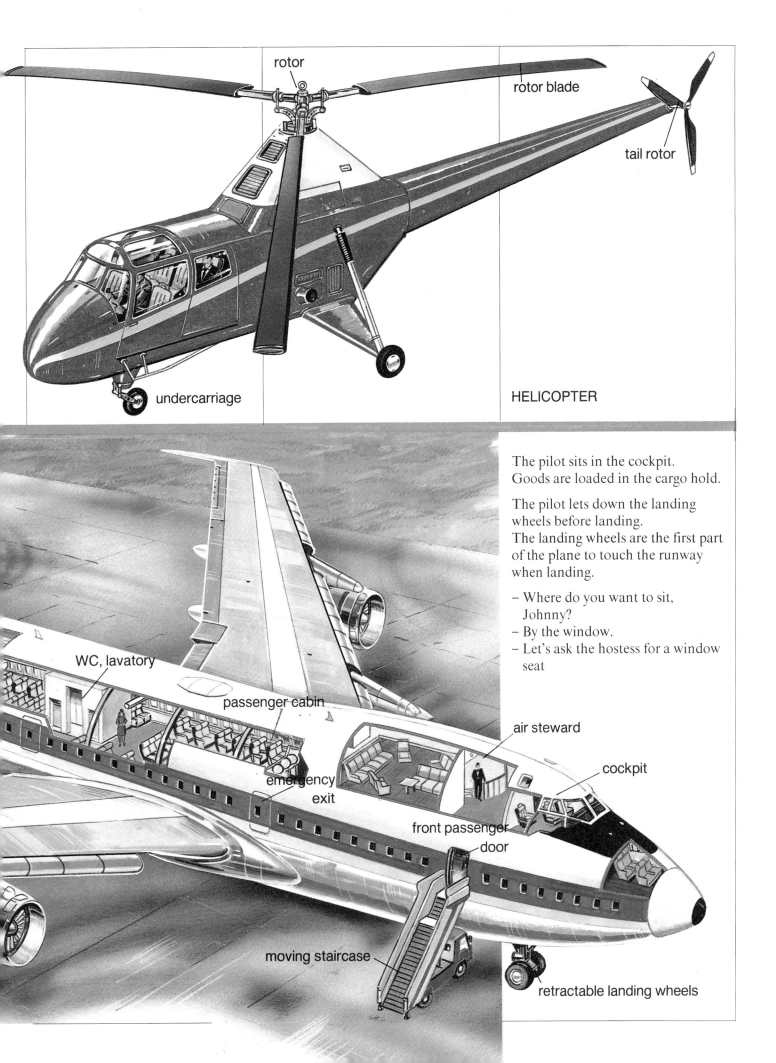

rotor

rotor blade

tail rotor

undercarriage

HELICOPTER

The pilot sits in the cockpit.
Goods are loaded in the cargo hold.

The pilot lets down the landing
wheels before landing.
The landing wheels are the first part
of the plane to touch the runway
when landing.

– Where do you want to sit,
  Johnny?
– By the window.
– Let's ask the hostess for a window
  seat

WC, lavatory

passenger cabin

air steward

cockpit

emergency
exit

front passenger
door

moving staircase

retractable landing wheels

45 THE AIRPORT

– Excuse me. Is this the check-in point for the 3 o'clock flight to London?
– Yes, it's here, checking points 1 and 2.
  May I have your ticket, please?
– Here's the ticket and this is my luggage.

– Oh! This case is overweight.
– Sorry. What can I do about it?
– You have to pay extra for overweight.

runway

ramp

apron

terrace

tank truck

service vehicles

luggage wagon

luggage lockers

GATE 9

customs

arrivals

baggage claim

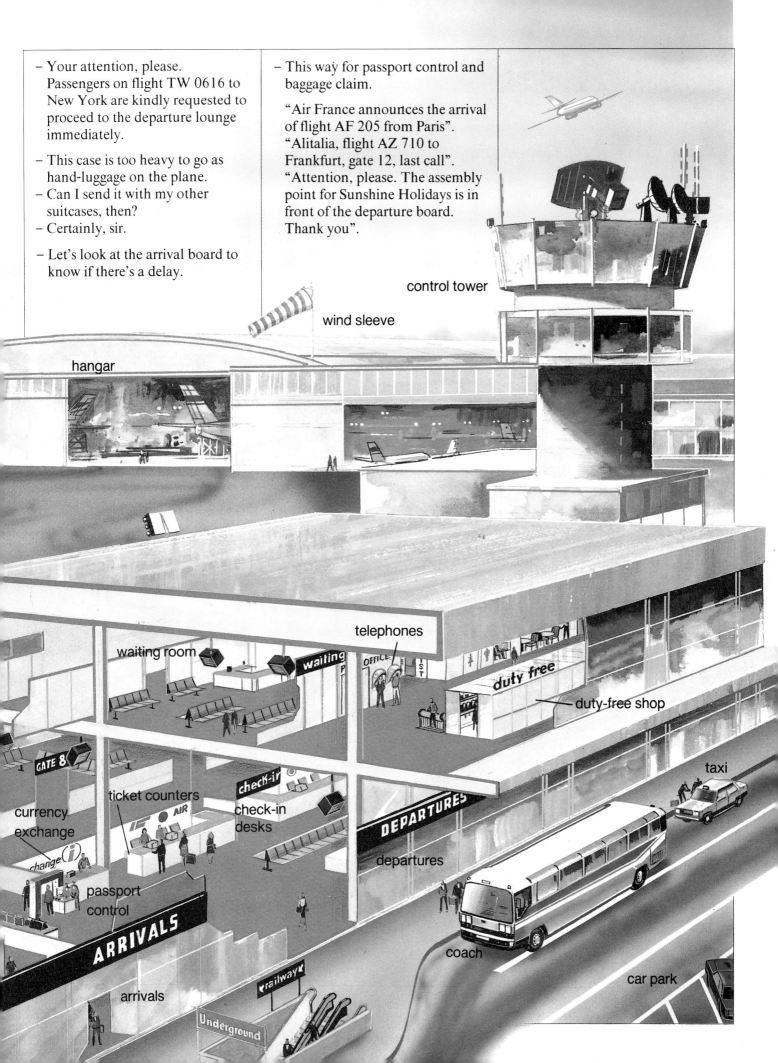

– Your attention, please. Passengers on flight TW 0616 to New York are kindly requested to proceed to the departure lounge immediately.

– This case is too heavy to go as hand-luggage on the plane.
– Can I send it with my other suitcases, then?
– Certainly, sir.

– Let's look at the arrival board to know if there's a delay.

– This way for passport control and baggage claim.

"Air France announces the arrival of flight AF 205 from Paris".
"Alitalia, flight AZ 710 to Frankfurt, gate 12, last call".
"Attention, please. The assembly point for Sunshine Holidays is in front of the departure board. Thank you".

control tower

wind sleeve

hangar

telephones

waiting room

waiting

OFFICE

duty free

duty-free shop

GATE 8

check-in

ticket counters

check-in desks

DEPARTURES

currency exchange

change

AIR

departures

taxi

passport control

ARRIVALS

coach

arrivals

railway

car park

Underground

THE HARBOUR

flashing light

liner

silo

lighthouse

periscope

floating dock

submarine

buoy

barge

radar

cargo ship

pier

DOCK AREA

(quayside) crane

tanker

container ship

tug

ferry-boat

container

quay

forklift

anchor

bollard

- What's the difference between a port and a harbour?
- A harbour is a naturally protected area, while a port is constructed to offer protection to ships.

- What other word is the word "quay" (Q-U-A-Y) pronounced like?
- It's pronounced like the word "key" (K-E-Y).
- Ships dock at the quay when they come into port.

- Tugs are small, but they help big liners to enter a port.

- What are cranes used for in a port?
- They are used for lifting heavy crates and loading them onto ships.

A lighthouse signals the entrance to a port.

47 A PASSENGER LINER

- The noise in the engine room is unbearable.

- What happens when a sailor suffers from seasickness?

- The swimming pool is off the saloon deck.

- The cargo was loaded before the passengers went on board. It is all stored in the hold.

- If you see someone falling over the rail into the sea, you must shout "man overboard" and give the alarm.

- This ship is flying a British flag.

- The captain is on his bridge.

- Dad, I want to open the window.
- There are no windows here, we're on board ship, John. Ships have portholes.

funnel

deckchairs

sun deck

swimming pool

poop deck

stern

rudder

ship's propeller

promenade deck

boat

engine room

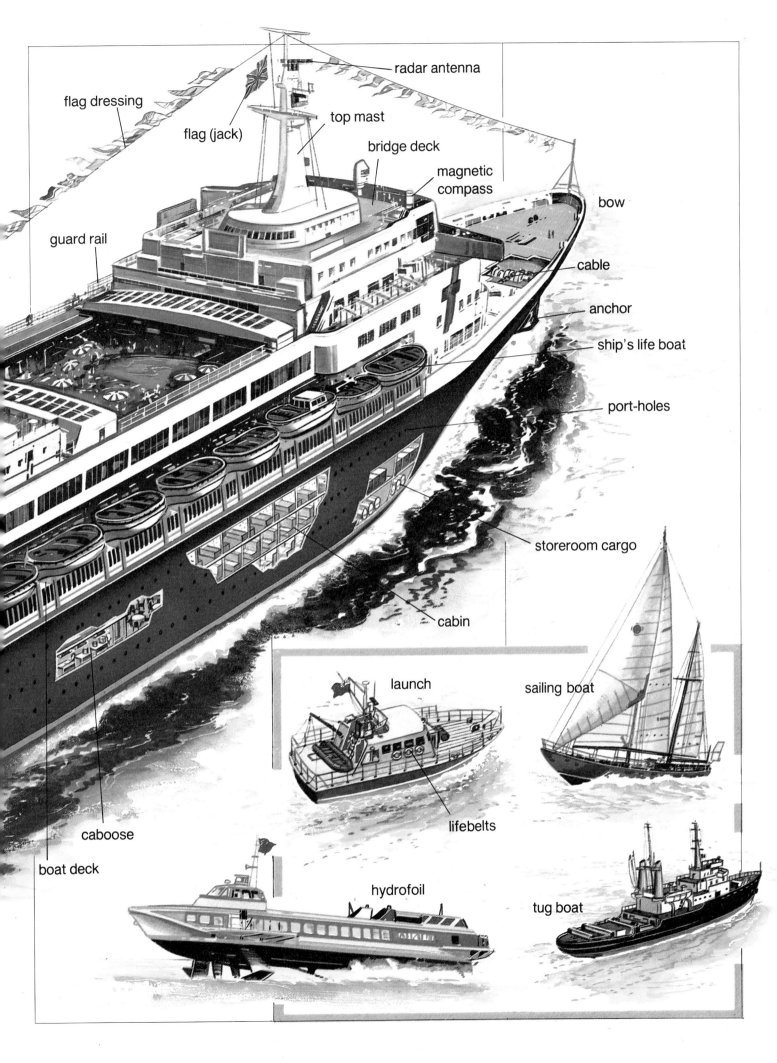

radar antenna

flag dressing

flag (jack)

top mast

bridge deck

magnetic compass

bow

guard rail

cable

anchor

ship's life boat

port-holes

storeroom cargo

cabin

launch

sailing boat

lifebelts

caboose

boat deck

hydrofoil

tug boat

48 THE HOTEL

– Please sign the register. The porter will take your suitcases and show you to your room. Here's your key.

– I'll ask the doorman to call a taxi.

– Shall we meet in the lobby at 9 p.m.?

– Are there any letters for me?
– Yes, here you are sir, and there's a phone-call, too.

– Would you ask the receptionist to prepare our bill, please?

chandelier

hotel bar

shaker

barman

bottle of whisky

ice bucket

cocktail

stool

waitress

sofa

armchair

ashtray

cigarette girl

lift boy

49 THE POST OFFICE

– When you want to buy some stamps you go to a post office.

– A postman collects and delivers letters and parcels.

letter
postmark
stamp
envelope
address
post-code
postcard
telegram
notice
string
parcel
label
hatch
clerk
scales
counter
rubber stamp
writing-paper
postman
(mail) van
letter box
mailbag

English stamps

Spanish stamp

French stamp

Polish stamp

Russian stamp

German stamp

telephone directories

telephone box

receiver (or handset)

cradle (or hook)

dial

cord

table telephones

microphone

earpiece

– Put the parcel on the scales, please. I have to weigh it. Has it got a label on it?... But there's no address on the label!

– Jennifer sent me a postcard from London. There's a red pillar-box on it.

– There's a telephone box outside if you want to make a telephone call.
Dial "O" to call the operator.

– The receiver was off the hook. That's why we received no calls!

– Some of the numbers on the dial are illegible.

– Oh! How silly of me. I was holding the receiver upside down, so I was talking into the earpiece and, of course, I couldn't hear what John was saying.

50 THE BANK

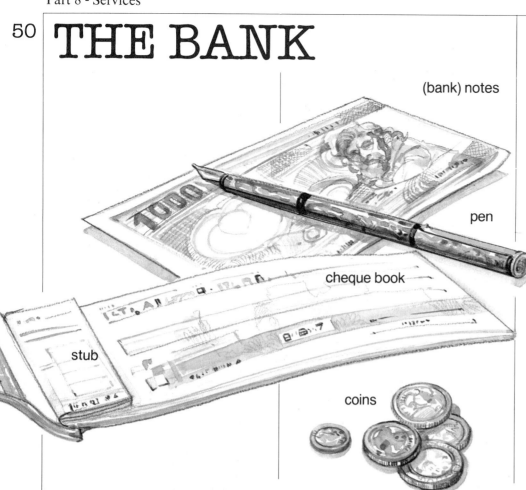

(bank) notes

pen

cheque book

stub

coins

- I want to change £ 100, please. How much will you give me in dollars?
- At today's rates you'll get 1,8 dollars for every pound.

- Why is the cashier in a cage, mum?
- Well, it isn't exactly a cage, but he's protected by bullet-proof glass. He won't get hurt if bank robbers start shooting.

- Customers' jewellery is kept in the strong room.

- I have some money to invest.
- Then you'd better speak to the manager. Come this way, please.

FOREIGN EXCHANGE

LIST OF QUOTATIONS

CASH DESK

bullet-proof glass

service counter

customer

strong room

strong-boxes

bank clerk

bars

STOCK LIST

cashier

brochures

half penny

one penny

two pence

five pence

ten pence

twenty pence

fifty pence

one pound

five pounds

ten pounds

twenty pounds

51 JOURNALISM

- Have you got a copy of yesterday's Times, please? I forgot to buy one and I believe there was a good article about Dante on the literary page.

- Jane, if you're going to interview Sting, you'd better take a tape-recorder with you.
- Good idea Tom, thank you.

- I always read the "Letters to the Editor"

- The Sunday papers often have colour supplements.

- The sub-editor edits articles sent to the paper and writes the headlines, too.

- If a magazine is printed before the proofs are corrected, it will probably be full of misprints.

- The editor wants his secretary to send a telex to New York. He's looking for information to confirm a scoop.

EDITORIAL STAFF

typewriter

shorthand typist

maker-up

microphone

reporter

tape recorder

interview

PRESS AGENCY

photographer

flash

camera

telephone

sub editor

telex

proofs

compositor

publisher

rollers

rotary press

news stand

weeklies

magazines

strip cartoon

OBSERVER

HOME NEWS

article

photo

banner headline

editorial

dailies

52 THE FIRE BRIGADE

– Help! Help! Fire! Fire!
  Ring for the Fire Brigade.

– They're coming. I can hear the bell.

– Look at the firemen climbing the ladder. They're wearing helmets.

– They've turned the hoses on the flames.

– The smoke is making me cough.

– Let's hope they save everybody.

fire

jet

mackintosh

foam

Wellington boots

asbestos suit

racing car

fire-extinguisher

ambulance

ambulance men

flashing lights

hydrant

helmet

stretcher

water

fire-escape

manhole cover

bell

smoke

fire-engine

ladder

hose

alarm siren

gas-mask

fireman

fire ladder

THE HOSPITAL

A HOSPITAL WARD

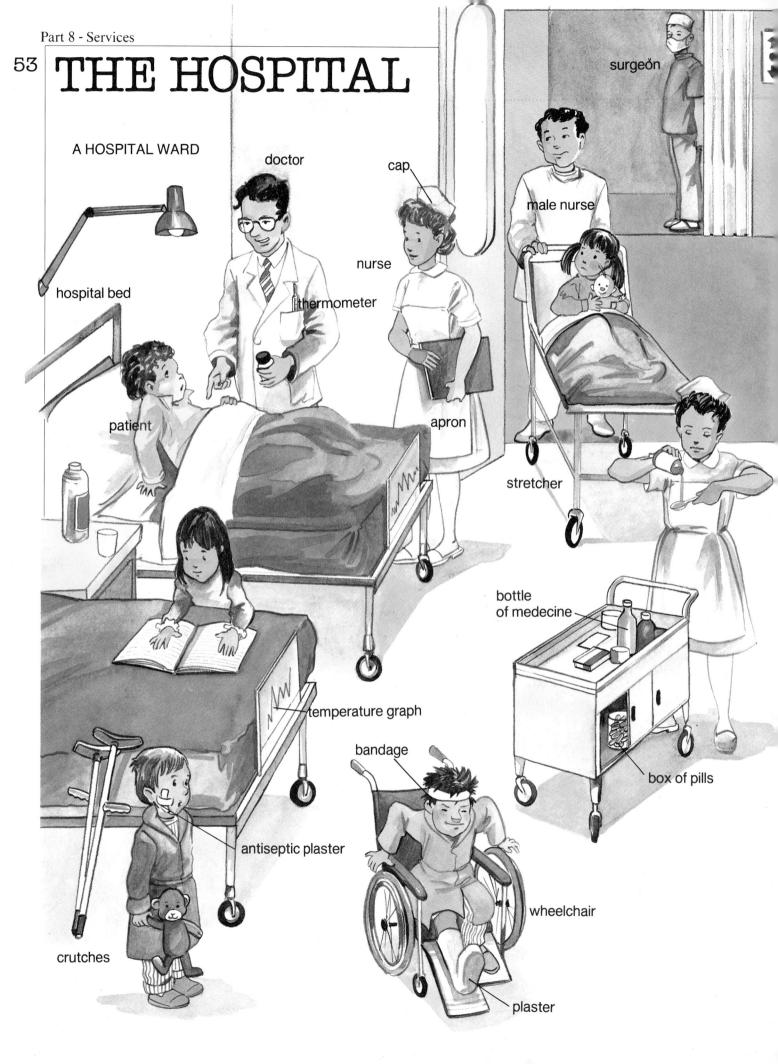

doctor

cap

nurse

surgeon

male nurse

hospital bed

thermometer

patient

apron

stretcher

bottle
of medecine

temperature graph

box of pills

bandage

antiseptic plaster

wheelchair

crutches

plaster

Sometimes there are 6 beds in a ward.

– I want to take your temperature. Put the thermometer into your mouth, please.
– Yes, nurse.

– Take this medicine twice a day before meals. Shake the bottle before use.

– Why did you have an X-ray?
– Because the doctor thought I had broken my arm.

– I'll bandage the cut and send you to hospital by ambulance.

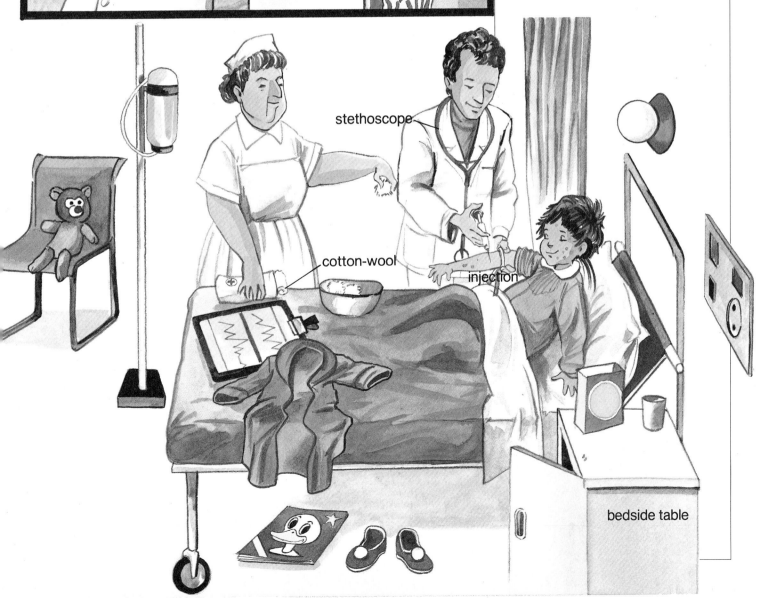

54 LAW AND ORDER

– Listen. What's that?
– It's the siren of a police-car.

– Sherlock Holmes always finds fingerprints that the police haven't seen.

– The judge, wearing his wig and gown, is addressing the jury.

helmet

uniform

policeman

police-dog

POLICE STATION

police inspector

witness

fingerprints

magnifying-glass

- The prisoner in the dock is not wearing handcuffs.
- A witness must always swear to tell the truth.
- The prison warder locks the cells every night.

jail (or prison)

cell

bars

prisoner

warder

police-car

handcuffs

prisoner at the bar

LAW COURT

wig

judge

bench

barrister

gown

jury

dock

55 NATIONAL DEFENCE

- Look at all those warships in the port.
- Yes, and look at that big one with the aeroplanes on it.
- That's an aircraft carrier.

- There's a monster coming up out of the sea!
- That's not a monster, it's a submarine.

jeep

rifle

pistol

machine-gun

bullets

cartridge

camouflaged cloth

- Let's play soldiers.
- All right. Ten soldiers and ten rifles for me.
- A soldier and a tank for me.
- A tank? All right; a fighter plane, a pilot and a bomb for me.
- ... I don't want to play soldiers now!

soldier

gun

grenade

tank

tracks

mortar

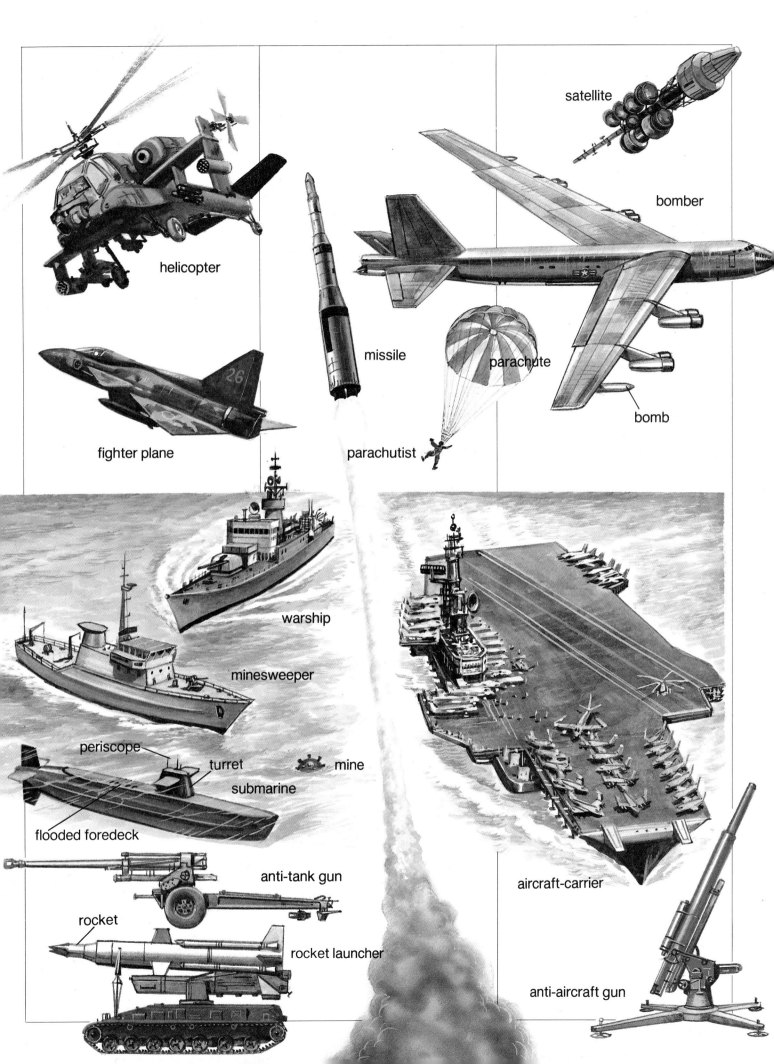

helicopter

satellite

bomber

missile

parachute

bomb

fighter plane

parachutist

warship

minesweeper

periscope

turret

mine

submarine

flooded foredeck

aircraft-carrier

anti-tank gun

rocket

rocket launcher

anti-aircraft gun

TIME

Big Ben

– What time do you get up?
– At a quarter to seven.

– If you go to bed at nine o'clock in the evening and get up at eight, how many hours do you sleep?

– Mum's birthday is in August and dad's is in March. When is your birthday?

– We go to the seaside in July.

– Christmas is on December 25th.

– If Sunday is the first day of the week, Monday is the second.

sundial

hourglass (egg timer)

TIMES OF THE DAY

midnight

night

evening

afternoon

midday

morning

cuckoo clock

watchmaker

alarm clock

waistcoat watch

- We have a sundial in our garden.
- There's a grandfather clock in the hall, but it doesn't go. Dad says it keeps him awake at night when it strikes the hours.
- What time did you set the alarm for?
- For 7.30.
- I never wind my watch. It's a digital one.

hour hand

(electronic) wrist-watch

minute hand

stop-watch

CLOCKS AND WATCHES

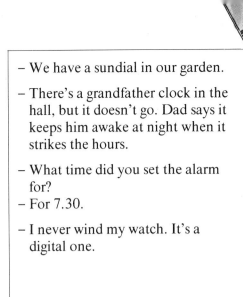

pocket-watch

(a) quarter to eleven

digital watch

face

PM **4** **15**

electric watch

pendulum

- We have lunch at midday.
- Before midday we say "good morning", after midday we say "good afternoon".

- We watch television in the evening.
- When I go to bed, mum says "goodnight".

nine o'clock

(a) quarter past six

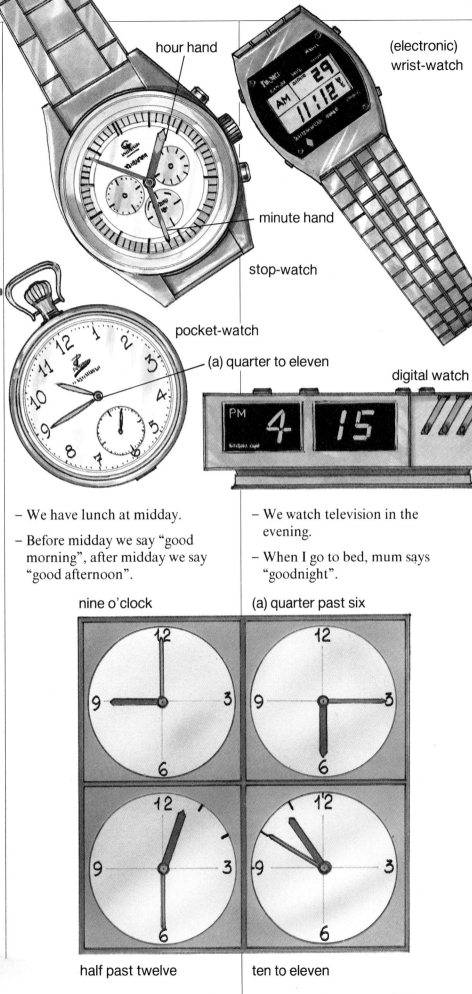

half past twelve

ten to eleven

grandfather clock

57

SEASONS

The days get longer and nights get shorter in spring.

In England, lambs are born in spring.

MONTHS
OF THE YEAR

March

April

May

June

July

August

June, July and August are the summer months.
We always go to the seaside for our summer holidays.

daffodils

lamb

swallow

butterfly

raspberry

beach umbrella

DAYS
OF THE WEEK

SPRING
21st March -
21st June

MARCH

Sunday	Monday	Tuesday	Wednesday	Thursday	Friday	Saturday
					1	2
3	4	5	6	7	8	9
10	11	12	13	14	15	16
17	18	19	20	21	22	23
24	25	26	27	28	29	30
31						

blossoms

hot sun

fruits

SUMMER
21st June -
23rd September

– Tom and Dick built a snowman in the garden.

They borrowed dad's pipe and stuck it into the snowman's mouth.

– Why are you so wet, Jimmy?
– We've been throwing snowballs!

WINTER
21st December –
21st March

snowman — February

snowdrops — January

Christmas tree — December

hibernation — November

roasted chestnuts — October

mushrooms — September

snow

slide

clouds

AUTUMN
23rd September –
21st December

some birds migrate to warmer climates.

– I like the smell of roasted chestnuts.
– So do I, but I like eating them, too!

Leaves change colour and fall from the trees in autumn. The nights get longer and the days get shorter and

leaves

58 WEATHER

After a heavy storm you can sometimes see a rainbow in the sky.

– I like wearing my rubber boots because I can walk in all the puddles and my feet don't get wet.

– Look at those dark clouds. It's going to rain.
Take your umbrella, if you go out.

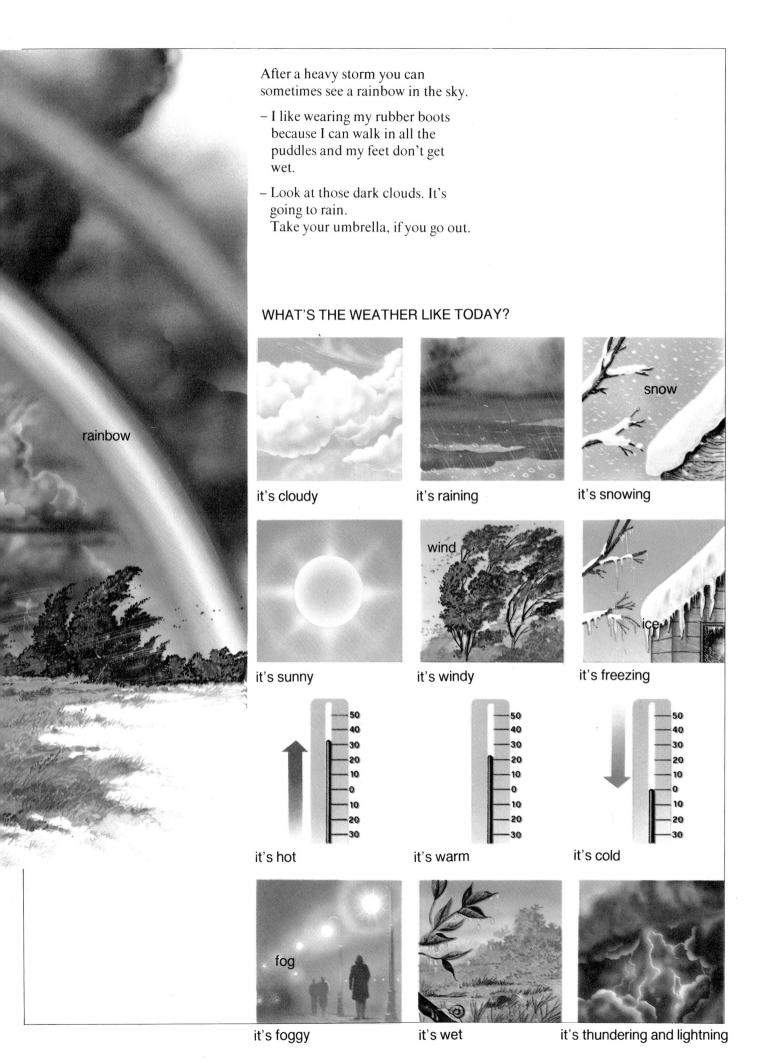

rainbow

WHAT'S THE WEATHER LIKE TODAY?

it's cloudy

it's raining

snow

it's snowing

it's sunny

wind

it's windy

ice

it's freezing

it's hot

it's warm

it's cold

fog

it's foggy

it's wet

it's thundering and lightning

OCCUPATIONS AND PROFESSIONS (a)

A nurse looks after sick people.

A butcher sells meat.

My dad goes to the barber's to have his hair cut, but my mum goes to the hairdresser's.

actor

actress

announcer

bank-clerk

barber

businessman

hairdresser

clerk

clown

sailor

tailor

driver

fireman

florist

footballer

We buy fruit and vegetables at the greengrocer's.

The waiter who served our lunch was so slow that the soup was cold.

When the lights don't work, we call the electrician.

I suffer from seasickness, I will never be a sailor.

When dad took his car to the garage, the mechanic said it was time to buy a new one.

architect

artist

baker

businesswoman

butcher

carpenter

waitress

dancer

mechanic

electrician

nurse

factory worker

gardener

greengrocer

writer

59 OCCUPATIONS AND PROFESSIONS (b)

- What would you like to do when you grow up?
- Either a cook or a grocer.
- Oh, why?
- Because then I would never be hungry.

singer

miner

secretary

vet

soldier

book-seller

plumber

doctor

pilot

typist

cook

priest

programmer

teacher

porter

– What do you do when you have a toothache?
– I go to the dentist's.

The chemist will give you the medicine that the doctor prescribes.

A postman delivers letters every day, except Sunday. Sometimes he walks, sometimes he has a bicycle.

A musician plays at least one musical instrument very well.

policewoman

grocer

seaman

postman

farmer

pianist

optician

shop assistant

photographer

dentist

baby sitter

journalist

policeman

scientist

musician

60 AN ARTIST

canvas

model

artist (painter)

brush

brushes

sketch book

easel

paint box

tubes of oil paint

turpentine

putty knife

water colours

palette

spatule

charcoal pencil

frame

The unfinished canvas was on an easel near the window.

An artist usually has a wide range of brushes, going from very fine to very thick ones.

An artist mixes colours on his palette when he wants a particular shade.

Most sculptors work with wood, stone or metal.

A sculptor uses a mallet and chisel to cut stone.

My grandfather painted that picture of my grandmother. He was a portrait painter.

David's new glasses are too big for him. They keep falling off his nose.

– Have you ever examined a drop of blood under a microscope?

– You're short-sighted, Mrs Brown. You need concave lenses.

A telescope is an optical instrument. So are binoculars.

An optician will tell you that the eye is like a camera.

– Dad says I must buy an extra lens if I want to take photos.

– I can't see anything.
– Move your hand, it's covering the viewfinder.
– Be careful not to move the camera when you're taking the photo.

– Let me take your photograph.
– Shall I say 'cheese'?
– Don't be silly. Don't pose! Just be natural.

– I bought a roll of film, but it's the wrong size for this camera.

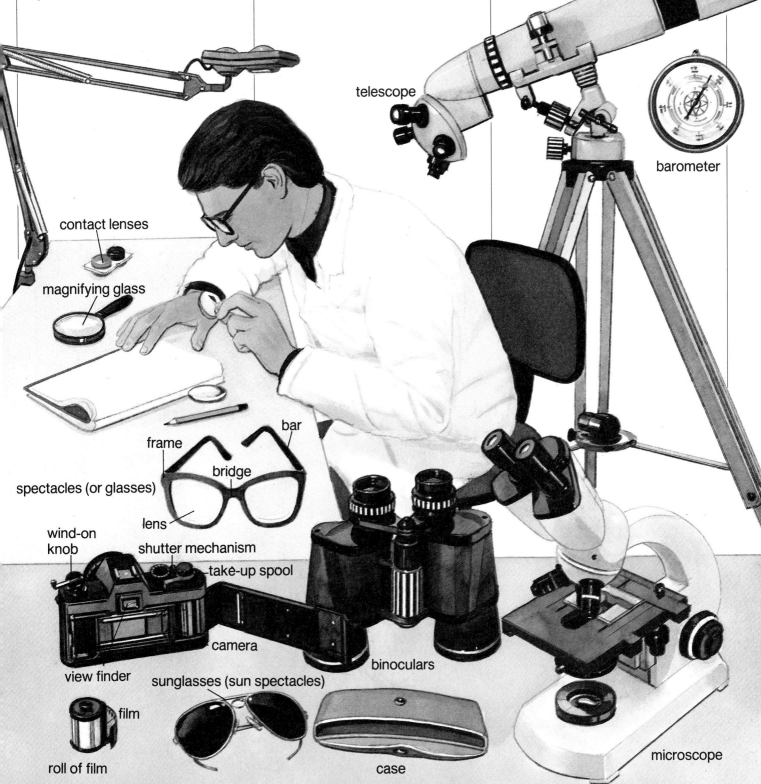

telescope

barometer

contact lenses

magnifying glass

frame
bar
bridge
spectacles (or glasses)
lens

wind-on knob
shutter mechanism
take-up spool
camera
view finder
binoculars
sunglasses (sun spectacles)

film
roll of film
case
microscope

A DENTIST

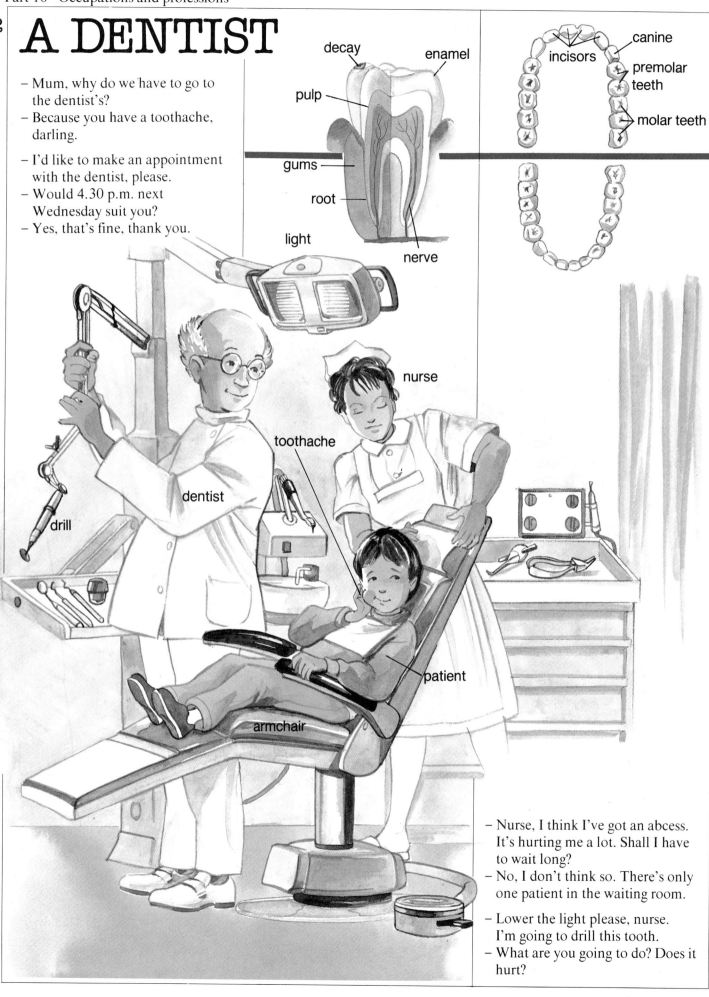

– Mum, why do we have to go to the dentist's?
– Because you have a toothache, darling.

– I'd like to make an appointment with the dentist, please.
– Would 4.30 p.m. next Wednesday suit you?
– Yes, that's fine, thank you.

decay

enamel

pulp

canine

incisors

premolar teeth

molar teeth

gums

root

nerve

light

dentist

drill

toothache

nurse

patient

armchair

– Nurse, I think I've got an abcess. It's hurting me a lot. Shall I have to wait long?
– No, I don't think so. There's only one patient in the waiting room.

– Lower the light please, nurse. I'm going to drill this tooth.
– What are you going to do? Does it hurt?

62

– Dad wants to hang up a picture.
Shall I get him some screws?
– Of course not. Go and get a
hammer and some nails.

– Can I borrow your saw?
– What do you want to do?
– Well, mum can't find her scissors.
She wants to clean some fish!

– Dad's electric drill is different
from the dentist's drill.

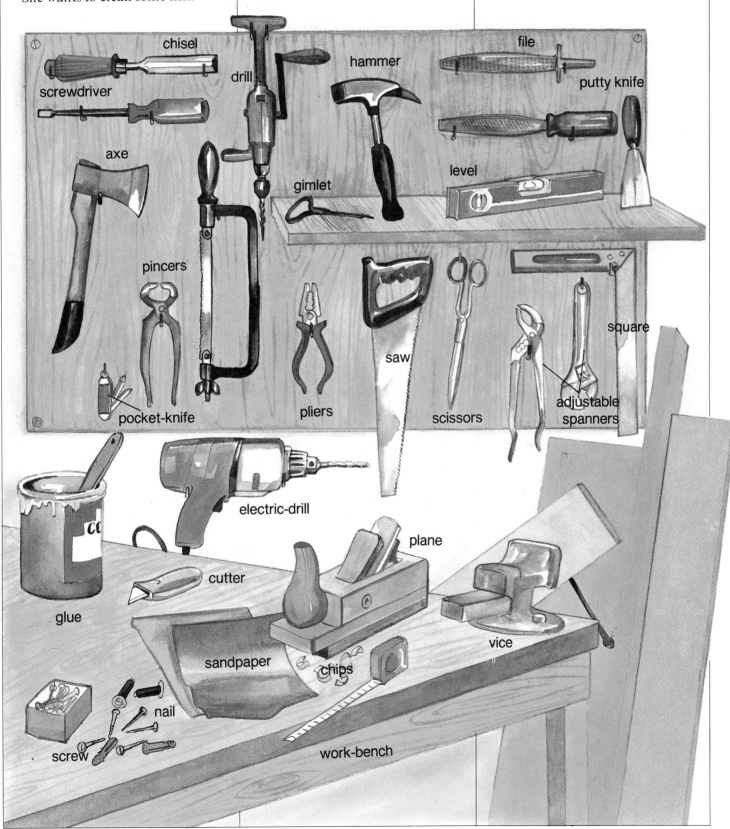

chisel

screwdriver

drill

hammer

file

putty knife

axe

gimlet

level

pincers

square

pocket-knife

pliers

saw

scissors

adjustable
spanners

electric-drill

plane

cutter

glue

sandpaper

chips

vice

nail

screw

work-bench

A PLUMBER

64

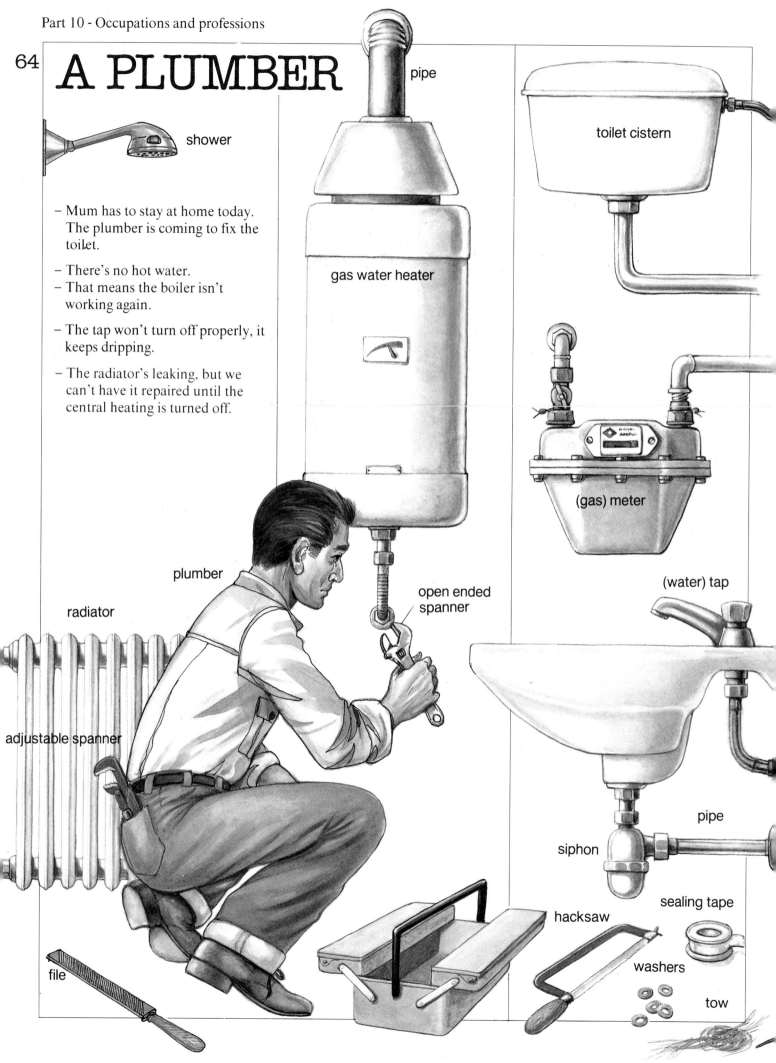

pipe

toilet cistern

shower

gas water heater

- Mum has to stay at home today. The plumber is coming to fix the toilet.

- There's no hot water.
- That means the boiler isn't working again.

- The tap won't turn off properly, it keeps dripping.

- The radiator's leaking, but we can't have it repaired until the central heating is turned off.

(gas) meter

(water) tap

plumber

radiator

open ended spanner

adjustable spanner

pipe

siphon

sealing tape

hacksaw

file

washers

tow

extension lead

light bulb

plug

socket

fluorescent tube

electricity meter

ABCDEF
Kwh 10590 15
CONTATORE 50A
220V

switch

pliers

wrench

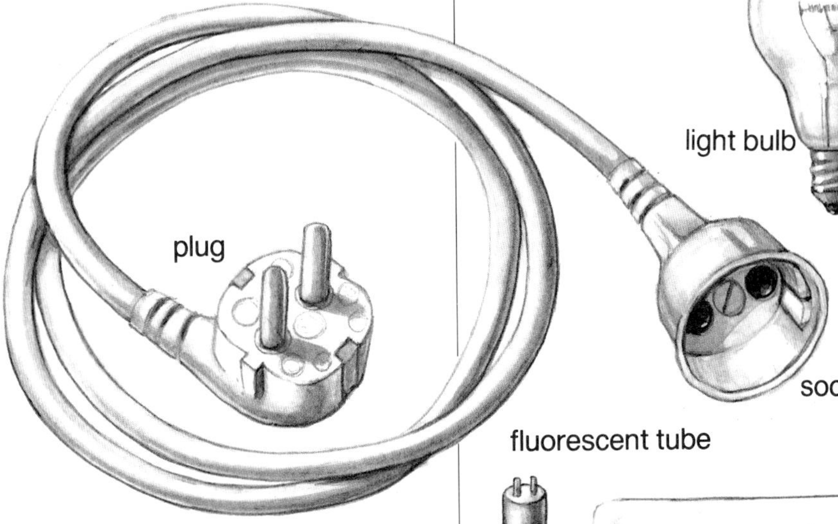

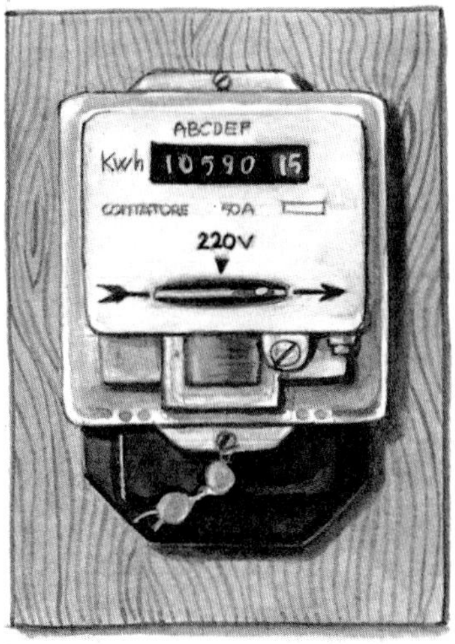

- Give the meter man a torch. He can't read the meter in the dark.

- Don't switch on the light while I'm changing the bulb.

- Put the plug in the socket, please.

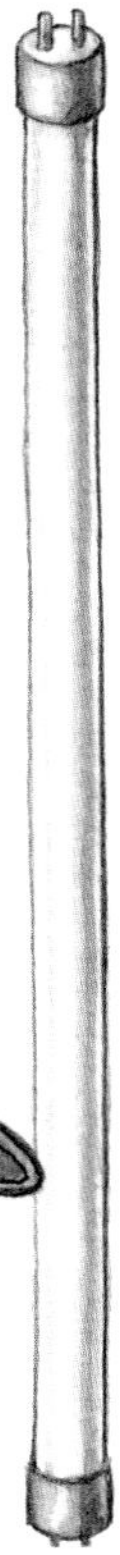

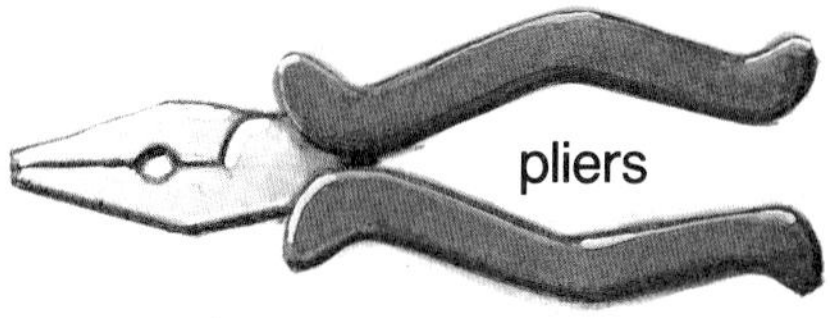

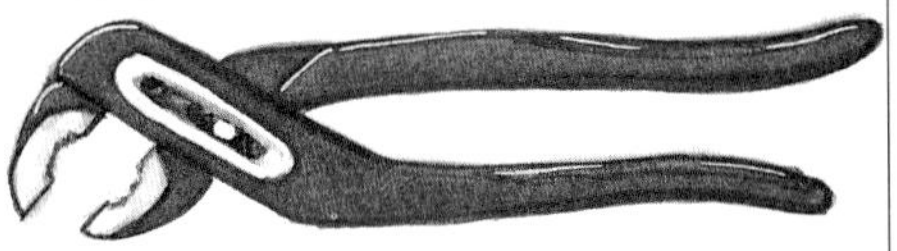

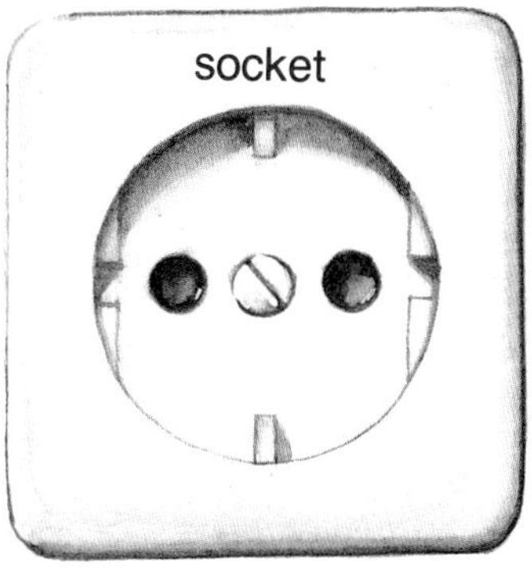

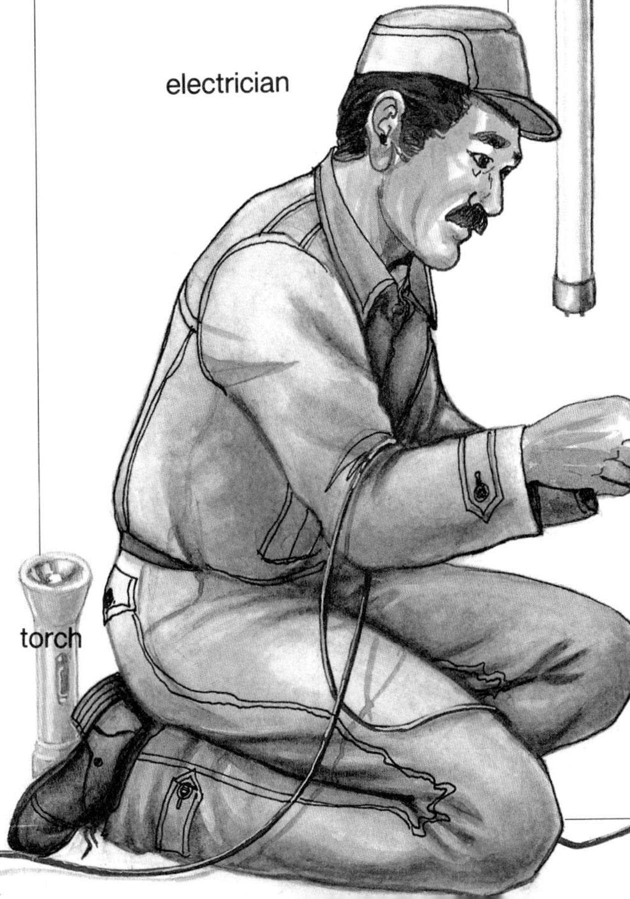

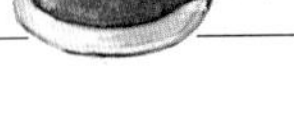

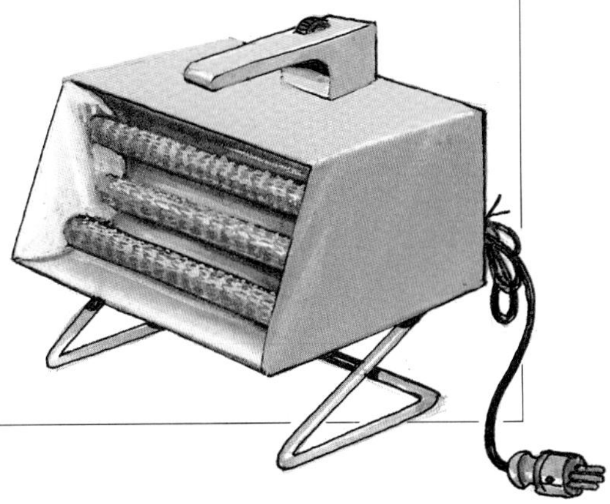

socket

bell

electrician

heater (fire)

torch

insulating tape

66

A HOUSEWIFE

- What does a housewife do every day?
- She cooks the meals.
- Does she do the ironing every day?
- Perhaps not.

- Do you make your own bed, Sam?
- No, I don't. Mum makes it for me.

- Who takes you to school, Linda?
- Dad does, but mum fetches me from school in the afternoon.

- Most housewives are pleased that washing machines have been invented.

makes the beds

does the washing

does the ironing

cooks meals

sweeps floors

vacuums

dusts the furniture

bathes the baby

takes the children to school

SEWING MACHINE

thread (or cotton)

cotton reel

needle

buttonhole

chalk

tape measure

scissors

safety pin

iron

thimble

button

pins

wool

zip-fastener
(or zipper)

elastic

knitting
needles

– This thimble is too small for my finger.

– You need four knitting needles and some wool to knit a pair of socks.

– If you don't sew that button on immediately you'll lose it.

– If your zip is broken, use a safety pin to keep your jacket closed.

– I can't thread this needle. I haven't got my glasses.

– Give me the needle and the reel of thread. I'll do it for you.

68 A PHOTOGRAPHER

When you have decided on what you want to photograph, you can focus your subject by turning the focus control

The flash gun fits into the flash shoe on top of your camera.

overhead light

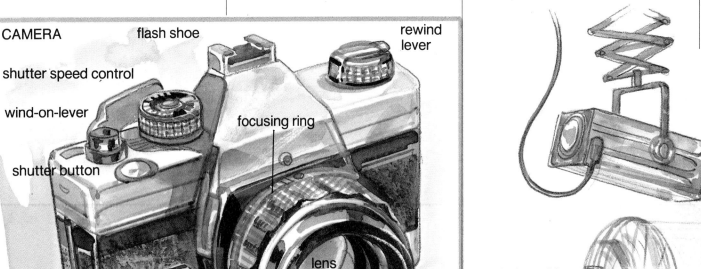

CAMERA

flash shoe

rewind lever

shutter speed control

wind-on-lever

focusing ring

shutter button

lens

focus control

wind machine

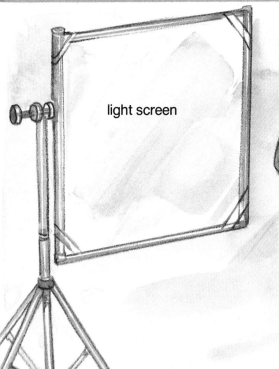

light screen

photographer

tripod

camera case

prints

exposure meter

telephoto lens

If you move the object you are photographing you will have to move the spotlight, too.

When the camera is on a tripod, it doesn't matter if the photographer's hand shakes.

When the safelight is on, it means that someone is working in the darkroom. You mustn't open the door.

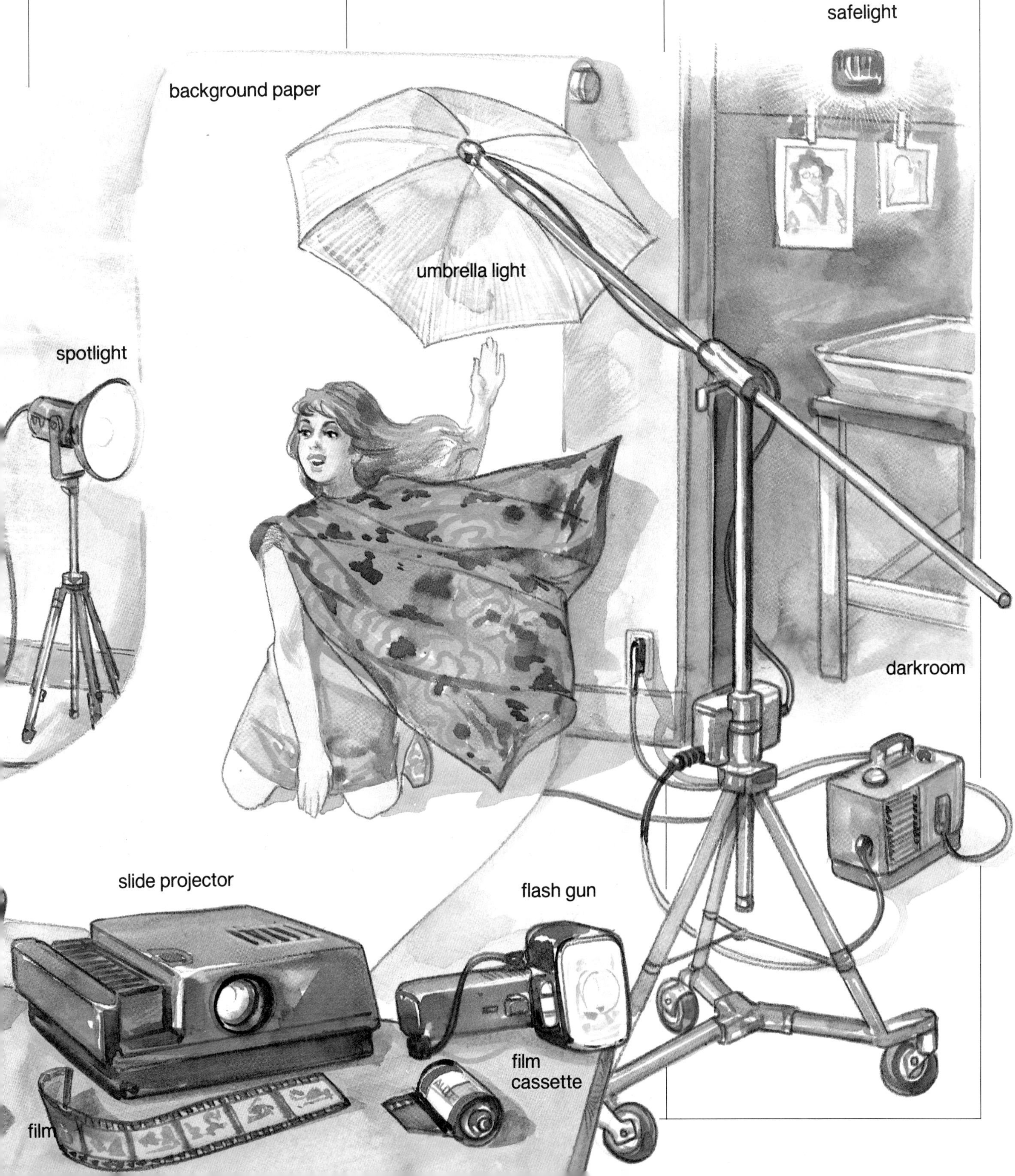

safelight

background paper

umbrella light

spotlight

darkroom

slide projector

flash gun

film cassette

film

69 OFFICE WORK

– My desk is near the window.
  There's a telephone on the desk.
  The typist sits near a window, too.

– My secretary writes down my
  appointments in my diary.

– Letters are filed in the filing
  cabinet.

– Hello, is that the operator? I want
  to call Italy.
– Hold on, please!
– Hello, hello!... operator... Oh,
  dear, I've been cut off!

– Miss Smith, you must be more
  careful! I've just found a £ 20
  note in your wastepaper basket!

A computer keyboard is more
complicated than a typewriter
keyboard.

Put some paper in the printer.

Take the disk out of the drive,
before switching off the computer.

A calculator makes arithmetic
easier.

When you ask a computer for
information, it will appear on the
screen in a few seconds.

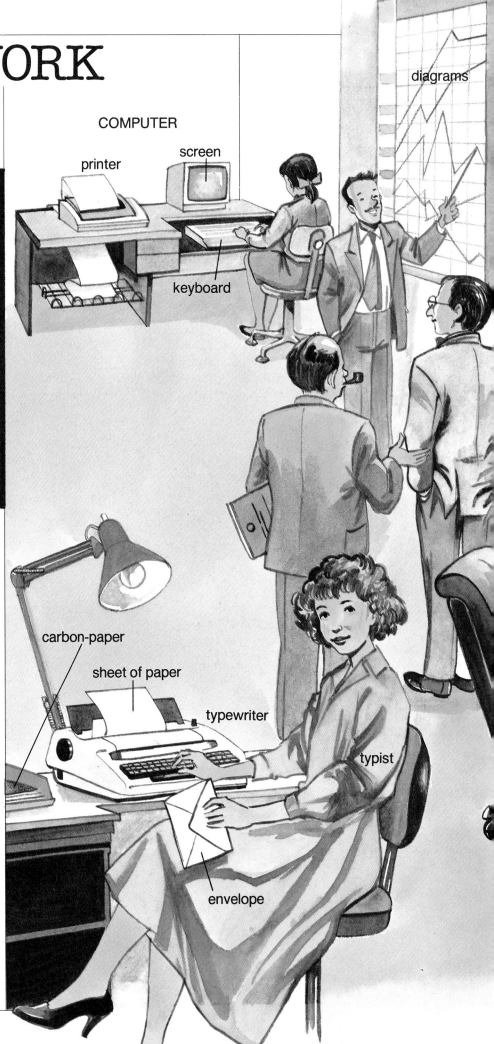

drawing board

knob

compass

T square

ruler

set square

(letters) basket

telephone

filing-cabinet

file

paper-clip

diary

hole-punch

stapler

calculator

desk

drawer

waste paper basket

PLANTS AND FLOWERS

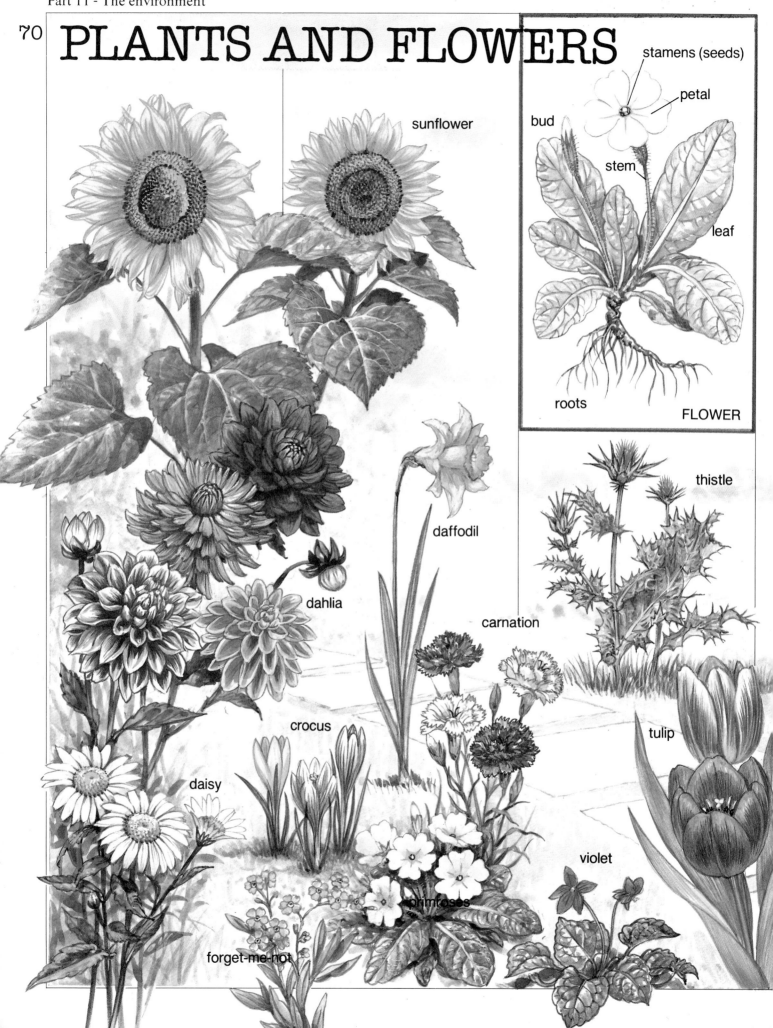

sunflower

stamens (seeds)

petal

bud

stem

leaf

roots

FLOWER

daffodil

dahlia

thistle

carnation

crocus

tulip

daisy

violet

primroses

forget-me-not

The thistle is the national symbol of Scotland.

Sunflowers always turn towards the sun, so they turn round during the day.

Children make daisy chains with daisies and hang them round their necks.

Banks of yellow daffodils are a sign of spring in England.

Primroses and wild violets often grow together.

Poppies grow wild in fields.

– Mum, this flower is for you with all my love.

– What does "forget-me-not" mean?

– It means that I want you to remember me.

lily

gladiolus

fuchsia

poppy

passion flower

geranium

rose

pansy

TREES

cypress

poplar

pine

larch

birch

chestnut (tree)

yew

TREE

trunk

branch

roots

leaf

(pine) cone

acorn

conker

horse chestnut

oak

magnolia

banana

willow

palm

maple

olive-tree

plane tree

When you plant an acorn, one day an oak tree may grow.

An old tree always has deep roots.

– We decorate a pine tree at Christmas, hang our presents on it and call it a Christmas tree.

– The yew is a coniferous tree, but the banana isn't.

– What is it, then?
– It's a deciduous tree.

– We can't eat conkers, but we can play with them.

ON THE FARM

cowshed

horse

cow

foal

calf

bull

pig

cock

chick

hen

goose

duck

piglet

sparrow

- Mum, do farm animals have a family?
- Yes, just like us. The baby of the cow is called the *calf* and the mother sheep has a *lamb*.
  All these "babies" have a special name.
- What about fathers?
- Well, the calf's father is called a *bull*, but he doesn't live with his family.

- In America, on Thanksgiving Day everyone eats turkey, because this bird was a native of America and saved the pioneers from starvation.

- On many farms there is a beehive where bees live a very busy life.

The cock crows early in the morning.

farmhouse

donkey

bees

kid

goat

sheep

lamb

turkey

mouse

beehive

rabbit

pond

ANIMALS that live in the FIELDS

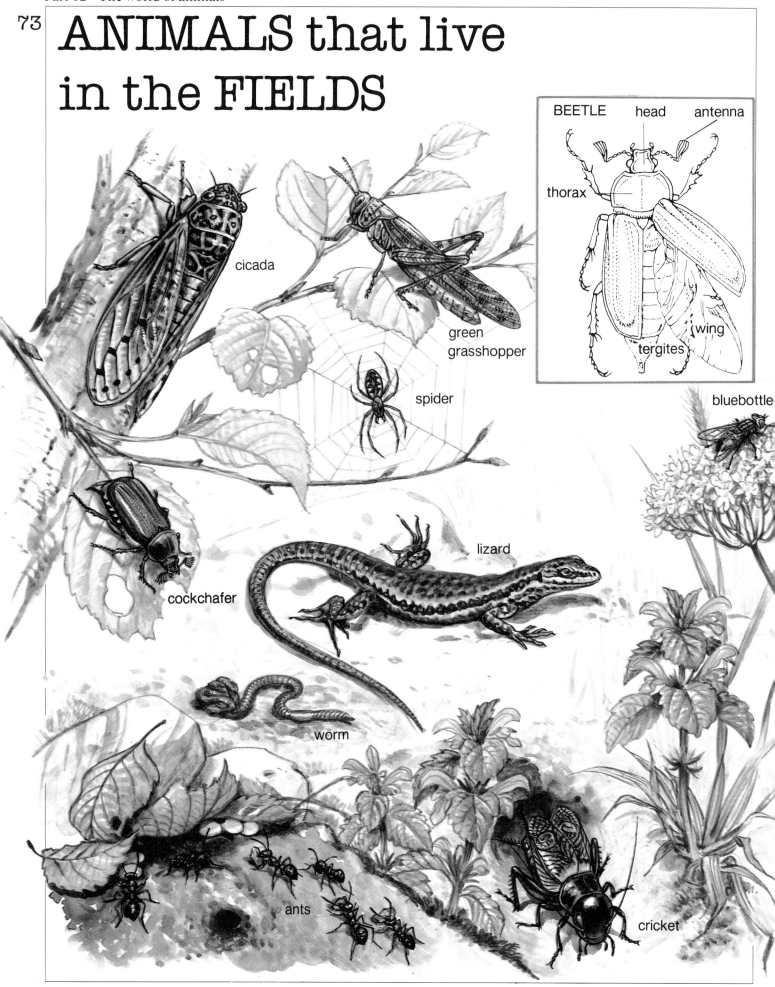

cicada

green grasshopper

spider

BEETLE   head   antenna

thorax

wing

tergites

bluebottle

cockchafer

lizard

worm

ants

cricket

midge

hare

mole

hornet

dragonfly

butterfly

bee

caterpillar

ladybird

mosquito

snail

Butterflies don't usually fly at night.

I didn't sleep at all last night because there was a mosquito in the bedroom.

Ants are very industrious insects.

Most spiders spin webs to catch flies and other insects.

– What do you know about bees?
– Bees make honey and they can sting too.

– Nobody likes black beetles and some people run when they see one.

– I like ladybirds because they have such pretty colours.
– They are pretty and they are useful too, because they eat harmful insects.

ANIMALS that live in the SAVANNAH

74

The lion is sometimes called the king of the forest.

They say that an elephant never forgets.

– Where did the zebra get its stripes from?
– I don't know, do you?
– No, I don't!

vulture

camel

elephant

termitary

ostrich

viper

crane

buffalo

kangaroo

hyena

scorpion

Antelopes are graceful animals with big horns.
They are herbivorous, in other words they feed on grass.

Grasshoppers have a short but active life.
They jump about and chirrup most of the time.

If a viper bites you, you should go straight to hospital for treatment.

– How many humps does a camel have?
– I don't know; two, perhaps.

The hares' hind legs are longer than their fore legs. This helps them to jump like kangaroos.

leopard

giraffe

antelope

rhinoceros

lion

zebra

lion cub

grasshopper

lizard

ANIMALS that live near SWAMPS

Crocodiles are strong swimmers and they like lying in the sun, too.

Have you ever tried to hold an eel in your hands? It's so slippery that it's almost impossible.

Salamanders are black and bright yellow.

Frogs have a smooth, slimy skin while toads have a rough, dry skin.

heron

hippopotamus

snake

flamingo

tortoise

salamander

toad

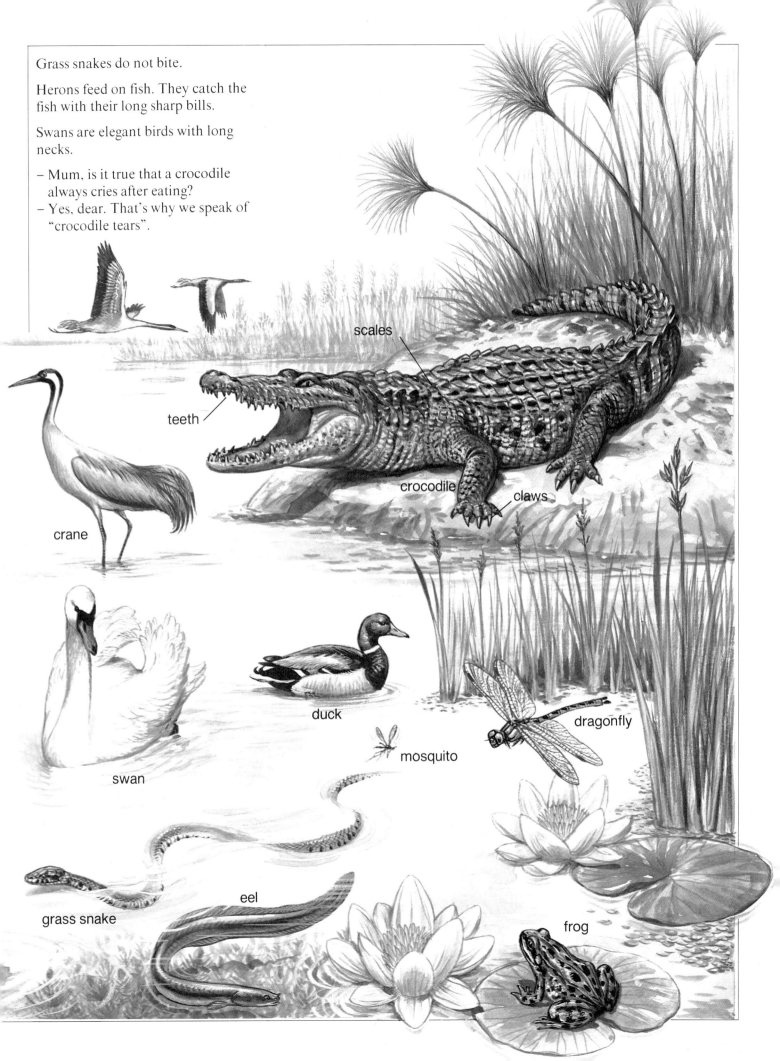

Grass snakes do not bite.

Herons feed on fish. They catch the fish with their long sharp bills.

Swans are elegant birds with long necks.

– Mum, is it true that a crocodile always cries after eating?
– Yes, dear. That's why we speak of "crocodile tears".

scales

teeth

crocodile

claws

crane

duck

dragonfly

mosquito

swan

grass snake

eel

frog

76

ANIMALS that live in the FOREST

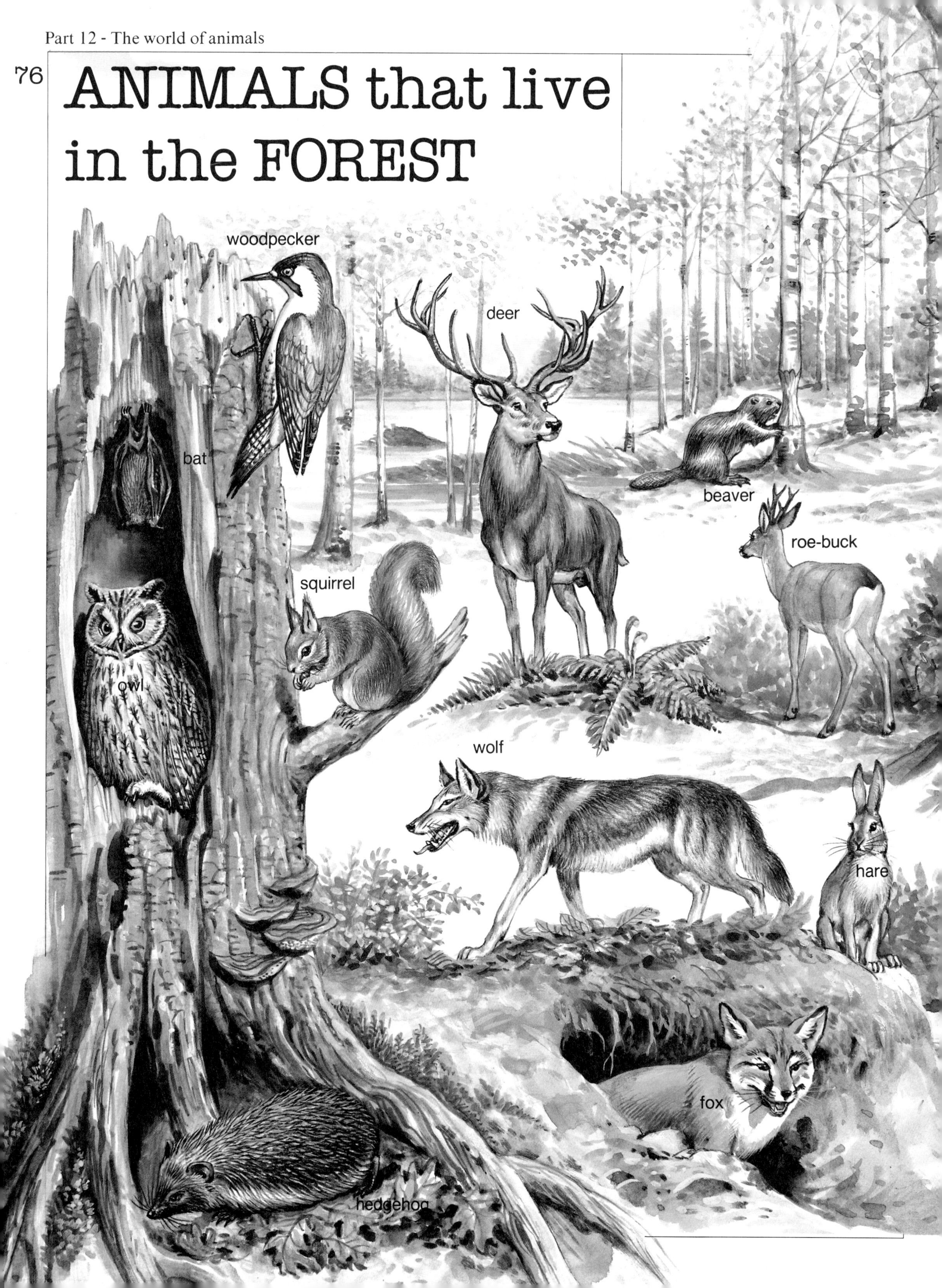

woodpecker

deer

beaver

roe-buck

bat

squirrel

owl

wolf

hare

fox

hedgehog

A lynx has very sharp eyesight.

When I see monkeys at the circus I wonder if my ancestors were monkeys.

My mum is frightened by bats. She says she's afraid they will fly into her hair.

horns

elk

reindeer

koala

panda

hoof, hooves

(wild) boar

lynx

monkey

jaguar

bear

tiger

snake

SKY ANIMALS

People say that owls are wise birds.

The dove is a symbol of peace.

They say that peacocks are proud. I suppose they are proud of their beautiful feathers.

The eagle is a bird of prey.

Swallows migrate from South Africa to northern countries in the summer.

Storks look after their young with great care.

Farmers don't like pigeons because they feed on grain.

eagle

swallow

hawk

condor

crow

peacock

stork

owl

toucan

parrot

nightingale

eggs

robin

blackbird

nest

SPARROW

beak

wing

feathers

claw

pigeon

dove

SEA ANIMALS

The prophet Jonah remained for three days in the belly of a whale.

There is nothing as slippery as an eel.

Jellyfish are pretty to look at but they can give you a nasty sting.

seal

walrus

penguin

dolphin

killer whale

jellyfish

sword-fish

eel

shark

squids

tuna fish

They say that sharks have poor eyesight but everyone knows that they definitely have sharp teeth.

Dolphins are playful animals. You can often see them jumping out of the water. They seem to be enjoying themselves.

– How many tentacles has an octopus got?
– Eight, of course.

– I know I'm going to catch a fish.
– How do you know?
– Well, I've got a crab to use as bait.

whale

mussels

turtle

oyster

sea urchin

shell

sea anemone

hermit crab

coral

sponge

starfish

lobster

octopus

crab

prawn

PETS

kennel

cereals

collar

fishfood

aquarium

goldfish

lead

tortoise

lettuce

dog

hamster

bone

puppy

– My goldfish swims in a big glass bowl all day and eats fish food.

Tony has a white rabbit in a hutch at the bottom of the garden.

Simon's tortoise is called Mr Slow.

Dogs like to bury bones when they have eaten all the meat.

Cats lick their kittens all the time to keep them clean.

Mum has two yellow canaries in a cage.

My parrot can speak English. It says, "Pretty Polly" "Pretty Polly"...

cage

guinea-pig

parrot

canary

stand

seed

cuttle-fish bone

cat

hutch

rabbit

kitten

carrot

bowl

PREHISTORY

Early man used sharp flintstones to make an axe.

Prehistoric men hunted animals using primitive weapons. They ate the meat and cut up the hides to make their clothes.

The Old Stone Age man drew pictures on the walls of caves.

In the New Stone Age, men polished their tools.

Dolmens can be found both in Great Britain and in France.

– What does the word "megalith" mean?
– It comes from the Greek word meaning "large stones". A megalith is a monument built with large blocks of stone.

axe

hunters

arrow

bow

throwing spear, made of bone

fire

firewood

hand axe

flintstone

basket

skin cloth

tusk

trunk

mammoth

flint dagger

dinosaur

pterodactyl

bison (cave painting)

cave

skin

amphora

stones

vases

PILE-DWELLING

hut

81 ANCIENT EGYPT

The river Nile dominated the early history of Eygpt.

The Egyptians built the pyramids as tombs for the Pharaoh.

The early Egyptian alphabet had so many letters or signs that only professional scribes did the writing.

Osiris, a mythical Egyptian hero, is said to be descended from Ra, the sun-god.

Papyrus was a plant growing on the banks of the Nile.
It was used to make a paperlike material more than 4,000 years ago.

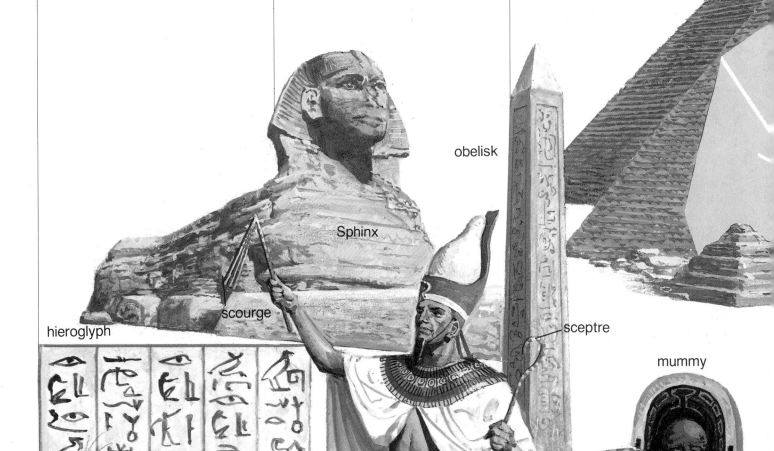

obelisk

Sphinx

scourge

hieroglyph

sceptre

mummy

papyrus

scribe

pharaoh

sarcophagus

PYRAMID, A ROYAL TOMB

king's chamber

corridor

entrance

The judgement of the dead:
While Osiris, the ruler of the dead, watches from its throne, the jackal-headed god Anubis weighs the heart of the deceased.

sun disk

scarab

lotus column

Geb, god of the earth

Thoth, moon god

Ra, personification of the sun at its zenith

Amon, king of gods

Horus, god of Lower Egypt

Isis, queen of gods

Anubis, god of the dead

Osiris, a fertility god and the giver of civilization

LIFE IN ANCIENT ATHENS

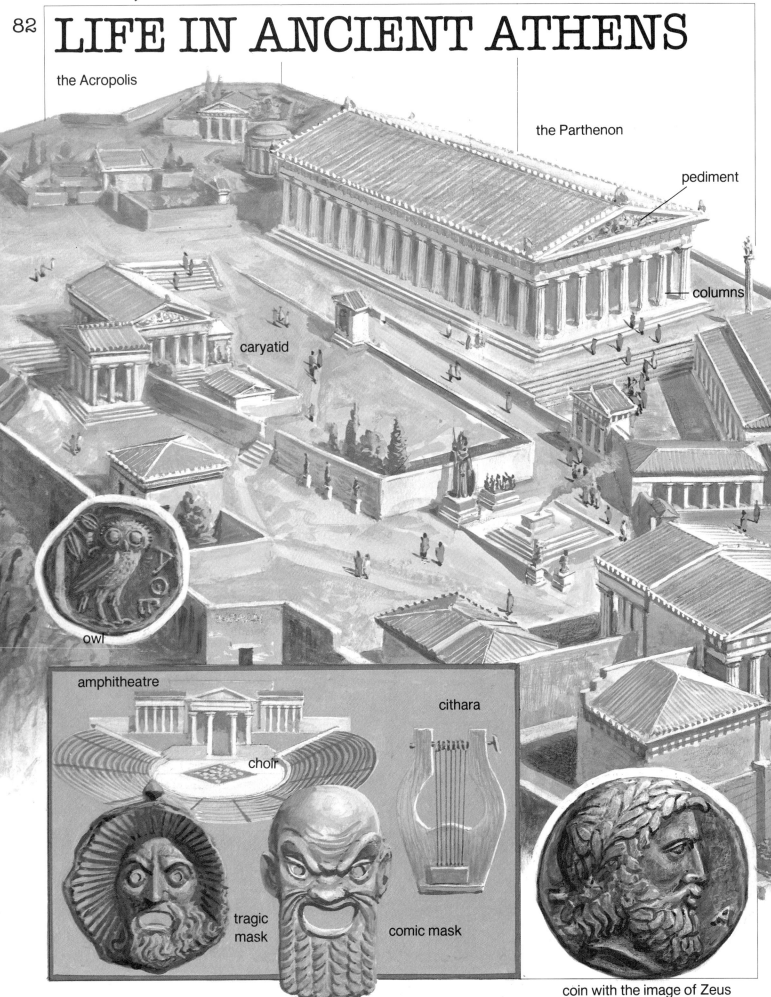

the Acropolis

the Parthenon

pediment

columns

caryatid

owl

amphitheatre

choir

cithara

tragic mask

comic mask

coin with the image of Zeus

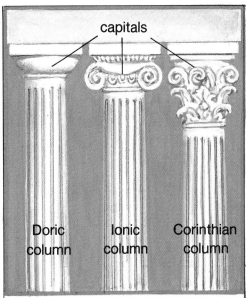

capitals

Doric column   Ionic column   Corinthian column

The goddess Athena was the protector of the city of Athens.

Tourists come from all over the world to visit the ruined temples of Athens.

A capital is the upper part of a column.
Different periods in Greek history are reflected in the design of capitals.

In a Greek theatre the audience sat in a semicircle round a circular stage, where a chorus danced and sang.

One interesting feature of early Greek drama was that there were never more than two actors on the stage at a time.

Greek temples were houses for the Gods, but they were not intended to house large congregations.

The first Olympic Games were held in Greece.

Socrates spent a lot of time in the market-place, talking to the people.

peplos

agora

potter's workshop

propylaea

statue of Athena

Greek vase

oil lamp

chiton

Socrates, the philosopher

THE ROMANS

Hadrian's Wall

The Roman legionaries were stationed along the frontiers of the Empire.

The ruins of old Roman bridges, aqueducts and amphitheatres are still to be seen in many parts of Europe and North Africa.

Ancient Roman senators all wore togas.

aqueduct

charioteers

legionary

armour

sword

girdle

centurion

chariot

fortifications

fibula

silver coin

GARALDI

toga

tunic

palla,
a coloured wrap

cobbled street

pottery

stola

helmet

spear

cuirass

dagger

shield

boots

foot soldier

– Do you know what they found
when they discovered an ancient
Roman tomb?
– No, I don't. Tell me.
– They found ancient pieces of
jewellery, necklaces and bracelets
and some old pottery, too.

– How many men formed a legion
in ancient Rome?
– Oh, there were certainly more
than 3,000 foot soldiers.

THE FEUDAL CASTLE

– Do you think a knight's armour was heavy?
– I don't know. Why do you ask?
– Well, it must have been difficult to fight with such heavy clothes.

– What happened when the enemy attacked a castle?
– The defenders drew up the draw bridge and prepared for a siege.

A powerful lord always protected his vassals when barbarians invaded the land.

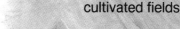

cultivated fields

village

flag

TOURNAMENT

helmet

knight

horse armour

cuirass

armour

lance

sword

were trying to climb up the castle walls.

There was always a sentinel in a watchtower.

If the water in the moat was deep, the enemy could not cross it.

The drawbridge was always raised when the castle was attacked, so that the enemy could not cross the moat.

Serfs were rather like slaves. They could not leave the land they cultivated for their lords, so they were not free.

The jester's job was to keep the lord amused.

Prisoners were kept in the dungeons of the castle.

Boiling oil was sometimes poured out through the loopholes, especially when the enemy soldiers

MAIN HALL

lord

vassal

jester

DUNGEON

prisoner

merlon

soldiers

bastion

loophole

tower

well

storerooms

serfs

courtyard

watchtower

front gate

drawbridge

moat

85

THE BUILDING OF A CATHEDRAL

– How different these churches are from the new churches of our city, mum.

– It's because old churches and cathedrals were built in mediaeval times. The building took years, even centuries. Architects, stone masons, sculptors, craftsmen of all kinds devoted all their lives to the construction.

– Mum, that window is round, not square.

– It's called a rose-window. All the pieces of coloured glass make a picture that tells you a Bible story. Let's go outside and look at the spires.

– They are like fingers - trying to reach the sky!

plan

architect

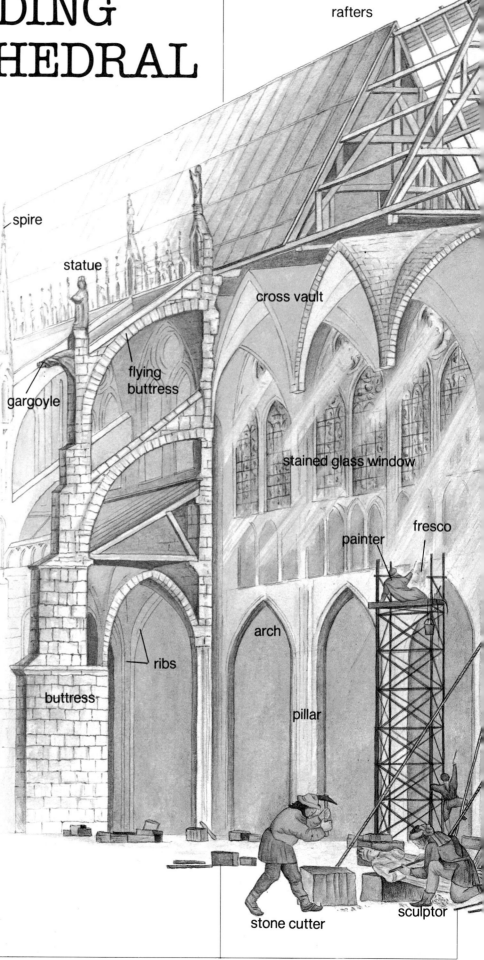

carpenter

rafters

spire

statue

cross vault

flying buttress

gargoyle

stained glass window

fresco

painter

arch

ribs

buttress

pillar

stone cutter

sculptor

pinnacle

rose window

tracery window

tympanum

facade

winch

church door
(or main door)

craftsmen

stone mason

cart

PIRATES AND CORSAIRS

The pirate flag is a skull and crossbones.
The pirates used to blindfold their prisoners and make them 'walk the plank'!
The pirates used grappling hooks to pull a boat closer to theirs, then they boarded it and fought with their daggers.

– Let's play pirates.
– All right. I'll be the captain of the pirate ship.
– I've got the map of an island where there's a treasure trove. Look - 'X' marks the spot.

– We've run aground. The island looks uninhabited.
Unload the barrels of gunpowder first.
Remember they must *not* get wet!

pirate flag

skull

crossbones

cannon

sabre

musket

dagger

pirate

Elizabethan collar

steering wheel

yard

sail

mast

cloak

unpowder

barrel

grappling hooks

brig

pistol

map

treasure trove

chest

CARIBBEAN ISLANDS

treasure

cannon balls

87 THE CONQUEST OF THE WEST

When Columbus discovered America, he was expecting to reach India. So he called the natives Indians.

The Indians living on the plains of North America used to hunt bisons or buffaloes. The buffalo's horns and bones were used to make tools.

caravan

pioneer

herd   guide   waggon

buffaloes

Other Indians used to hunt reindeer. They dried the meat and stored it in fat.

When they were hunting, the Indians lived in wigwams made of the bark of trees or in tepees made of buffalo skins.

sheriff

bridle

saddle

witch doctor

spur

stirrup

fire

ritual dance

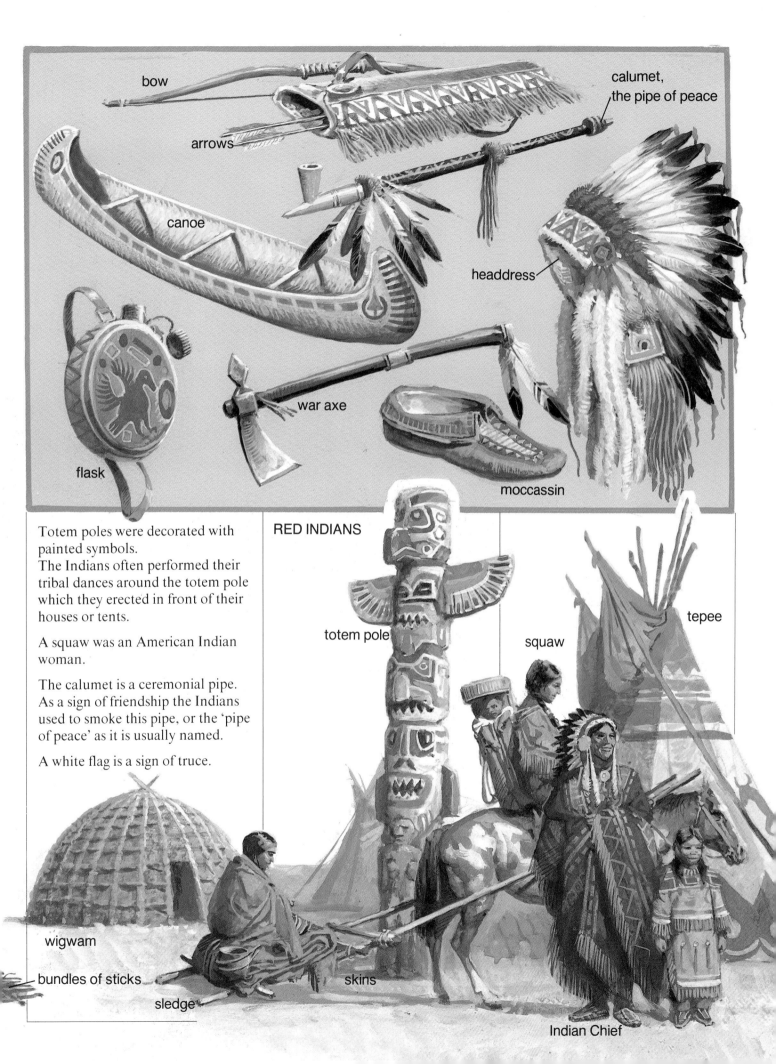

bow

arrows

calumet,
the pipe of peace

canoe

headdress

flask

war axe

moccassin

RED INDIANS

Totem poles were decorated with painted symbols.
The Indians often performed their tribal dances around the totem pole which they erected in front of their houses or tents.

A squaw was an American Indian woman.

The calumet is a ceremonial pipe. As a sign of friendship the Indians used to smoke this pipe, or the 'pipe of peace' as it is usually named.

A white flag is a sign of truce.

totem pole

squaw

tepee

wigwam

bundles of sticks

sledge

skins

Indian Chief

88 ON THE MOON

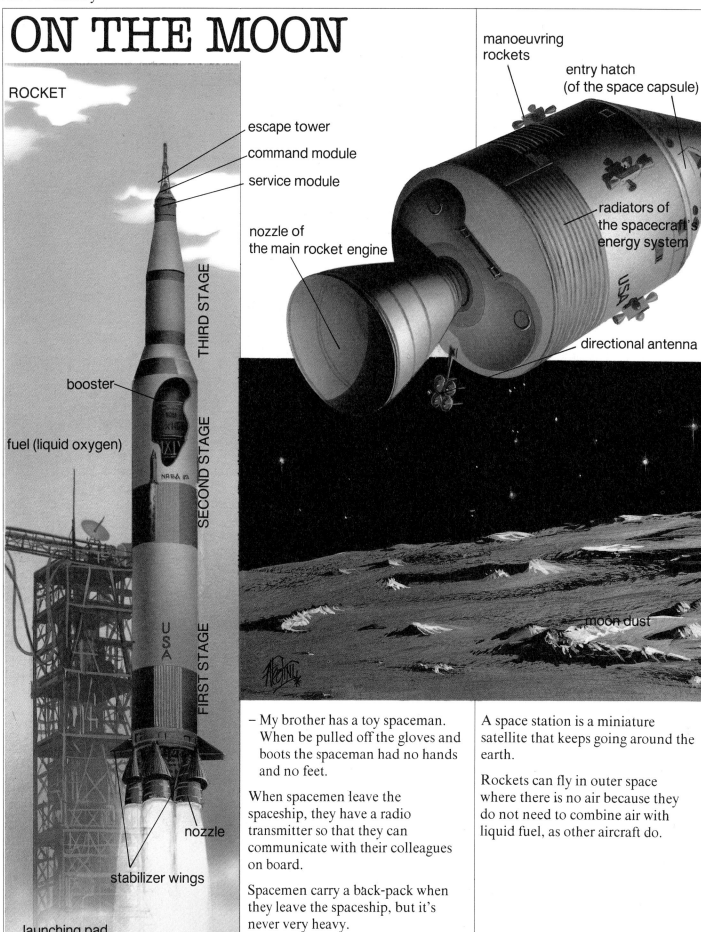

ROCKET

escape tower
command module
service module

THIRD STAGE

booster

fuel (liquid oxygen)

SECOND STAGE

nozzle of
the main rocket engine

FIRST STAGE

USA

nozzle

stabilizer wings

launching pad

manoeuvring
rockets

entry hatch
(of the space capsule)

radiators of
the spacecraft's
energy system

USA

directional antenna

moon dust

– My brother has a toy spaceman.
When be pulled off the gloves and
boots the spaceman had no hands
and no feet.

When spacemen leave the
spaceship, they have a radio
transmitter so that they can
communicate with their colleagues
on board.

Spacemen carry a back-pack when
they leave the spaceship, but it's
never very heavy.

A spaceman's helmet is like a
diver's helmet.

A space station is a miniature
satellite that keeps going around the
earth.

Rockets can fly in outer space
where there is no air because they
do not need to combine air with
liquid fuel, as other aircraft do.

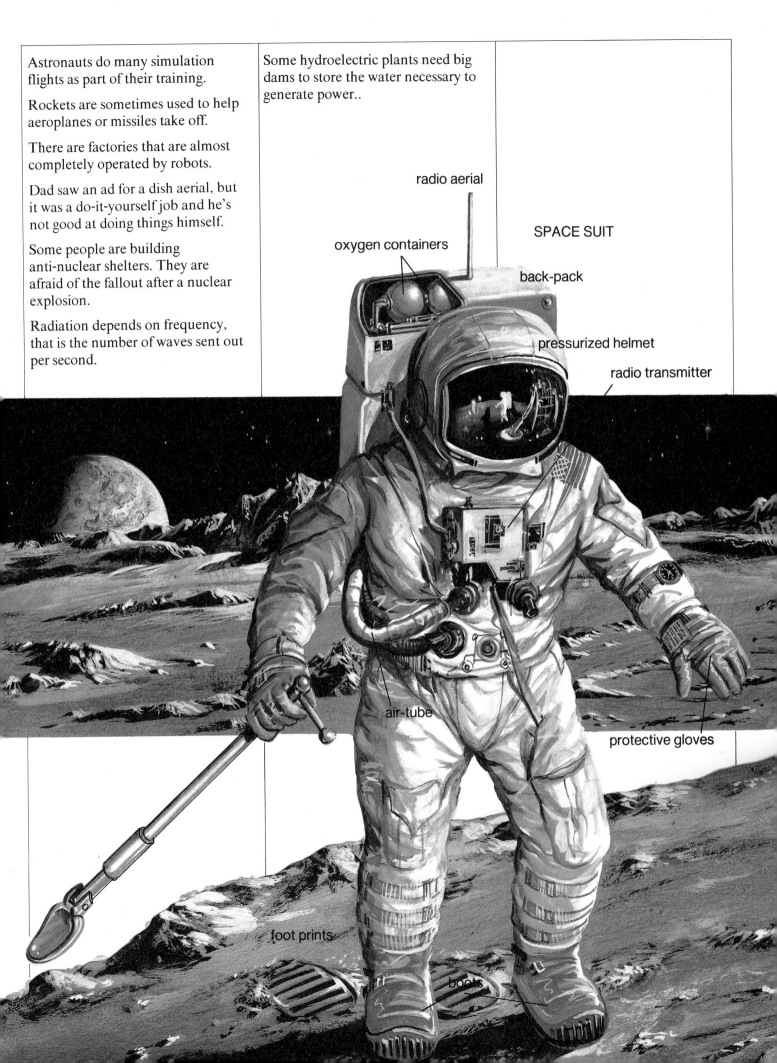

Astronauts do many simulation flights as part of their training.

Rockets are sometimes used to help aeroplanes or missiles take off.

There are factories that are almost completely operated by robots.

Dad saw an ad for a dish aerial, but it was a do-it-yourself job and he's not good at doing things himself.

Some people are building anti-nuclear shelters. They are afraid of the fallout after a nuclear explosion.

Radiation depends on frequency, that is the number of waves sent out per second.

Some hydroelectric plants need big dams to store the water necessary to generate power..

SPACE SUIT

radio aerial

oxygen containers

back-pack

pressurized helmet

radio transmitter

air-tube

protective gloves

foot prints

boots

HOBBIES

– Is cooking a hobby, mum?
– It is, but it can also be a profession.

– Playing computer games is great fun.
– Is it? I like watching films better.

camping

listening to music

collecting coins

playing computer games

taking photographs

cooking

singing

dancing

gardening

– I took a lot a photos last summer.
– Will you show them to me?
– I can't. You see, I forgot to put a film in my camera.

– Do you like reading, Bill?
– No, I don't. But I like the books granny gives me because they have a lot of pictures.

making models

reading

painting pictures

going to the theatre

playing the piano

watching films

jogging

fishing

knitting

TOYS

- My brother is learning to ride a bicycle, but he keeps falling off.
- Margaret's doll is too big for her doll's house.

- It's too windy today. I can't fly my kite.
- Tommy won't go to sleep without his teddy bear.

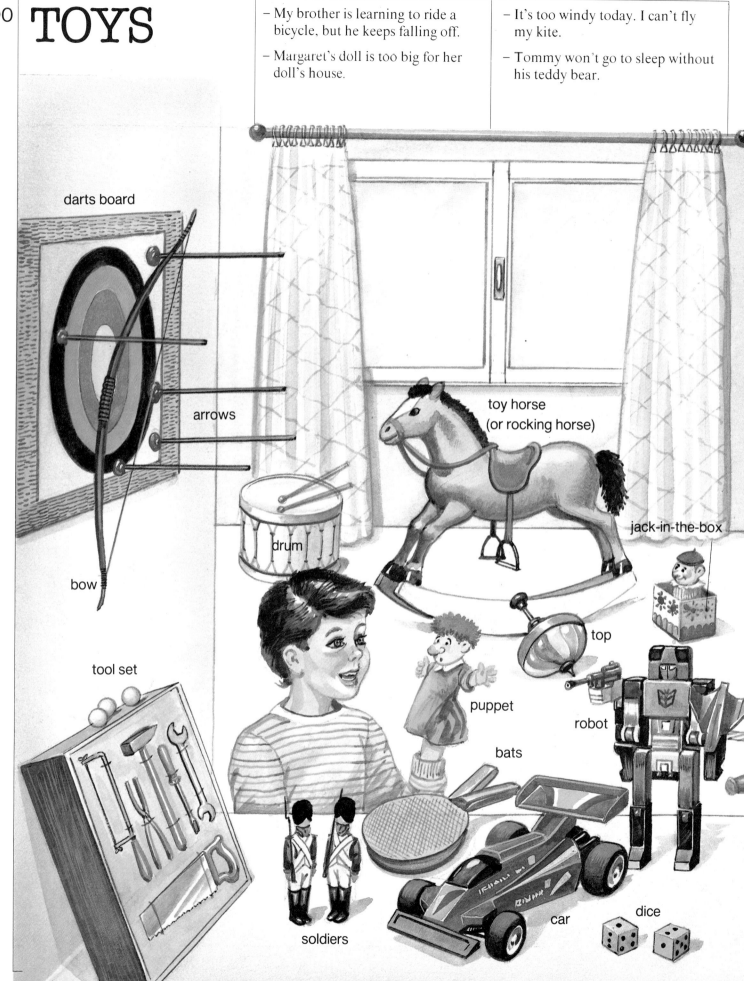

darts board

arrows

bow

tool set

drum

toy horse
(or rocking horse)

jack-in-the-box

top

puppet

robot

bats

soldiers

car

dice

– What do you want for Christmas?
– I want a bow and arrow like
  Robin Hood and I want a walkie-
  talkie like a policeman.

mask

castle

plane

piggy-bank

doll

doll's house

puzzle

soft toy (or cuddly toy)

bricks

marbles

skipping rope

train

whistle

teddy bear

colouring book

91 FAIRY TALES

witch

broom

– What is a fairy tale?
– It's a story about a fantasy world, where fairies and gnomes and other magic creatures live.

– Why do grown-ups tell children fairy tales?
– To amuse them, but also to teach them.

Cinderella has this name because her wicked step-mother made her sit near the cinders of the fire. Her good fairy protected her and helped her and her story had a very happy ending.

Little Red Riding Hood was a good little girl who took a basket of food to her old grandmother, in a cottage, in a forest. There was a wolf in her grandmother's bed, but this story also has a happy ending.

Pinocchio was a wooden puppet. Everytime he told a lie, his nose became longer and longer.

Many fairy stories begin with the words "Once upon a time" and they almost always end "... and they lived happily ever after".

stagecoach

wand

fairy

flute

Cinderella

mice

pumpkin

dragon

knight

beanstalk

Jack

mushrooms

gnome

magician

PUSS-IN-BOOTS

ogre

cat

boots

HANSEL AND GRETEL

the gingerbread house

SNOW WHITE

dwarf

PINOCCHIO

donkey ears

nose

wolf

RED RIDING HOOD

Mad Hatter

ALICE IN WONDERLAND

IN THE PARK

Andrew is flying his kite and Elizabeth is on the swing. Mum is pushing their baby brother down the slide.

– I can jump higher than you, Patrick.
– Yes. But I can run faster than you.

walkie-talkie

kite

hoop

bench

bowls

football

to run

to play football

scooter

skate board

roller skates

boat

– Let's go on the seesaw. Come on, Philip.
– Let's play tennis.
– I've got a racket but I haven't any tennis balls.

climbing frame

to fly a kite

bicycle

swing

to jump

slide

kipping ope

racket

seesaw

tennis court

net

tennis-ball

service line

93 GAMES

– How many cards are there in a pack, 52 or 54?
– There are 54, if you count the jokers.

– Can you play chess?
– No, I can play draughts but chess is too complicated.

– A Jack is a playing card with the picture of a man on it and a rank between the ten and the Queen.

chess

(set of) chessmen

board

king   queen   bishop   knight   castle   pawn

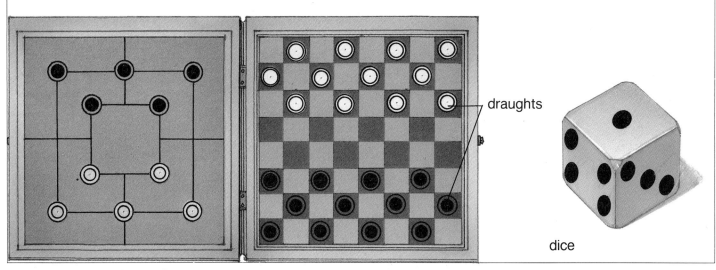

draughts

dice

nine men's morris   draught

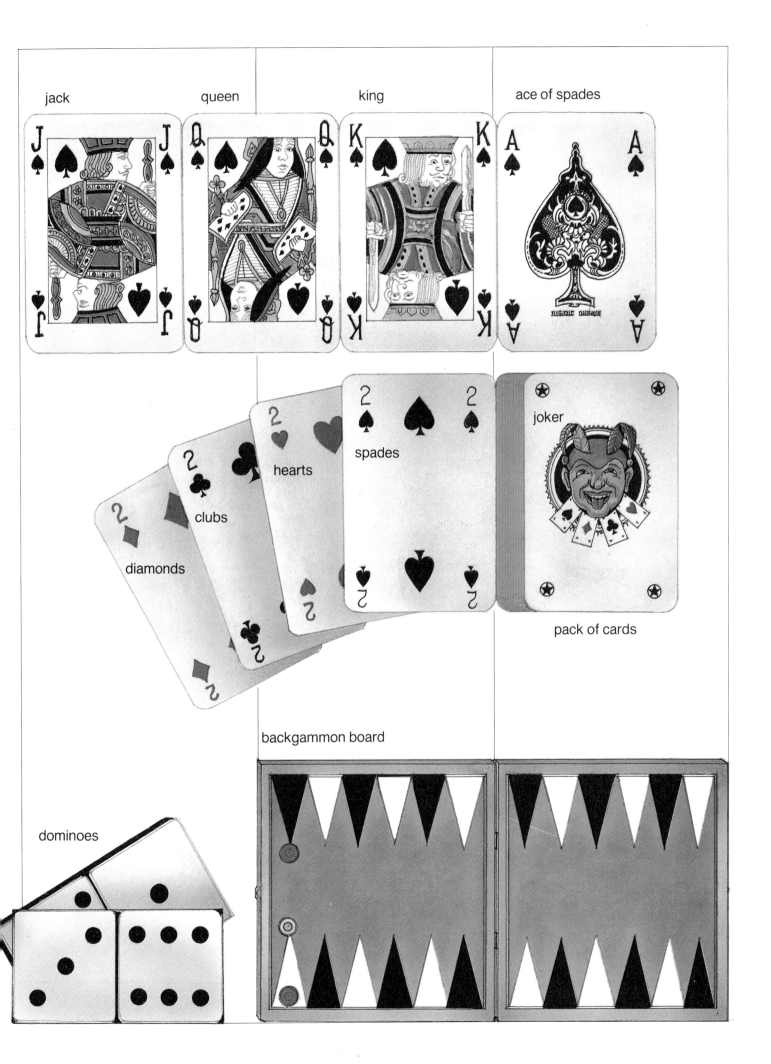

jack

queen

king

ace of spades

diamonds

clubs

hearts

spades

joker

pack of cards

backgammon board

dominoes

ATHLETICS

John prefers to run in relay races because they are team events.

Pole vaulting look easy, but perhaps it's easier to do the long jump.

Throwing the hammer is a sport where the competitors throw a metal ball, not a hammer.

A marathon is a very long race and sometimes hundreds of people take part.

stand

hammer throw

obstacle race (or steeplechase)

obstacle

running

pole vault

pole

starting block

running track

– How far did Michael jump the last time?
– 5 foot 4 inches.
– Is that a record?
– I don't know, but I don't think so.

the discus

shot put

long jump

sand

landing area

springboard

lane

marathon

bar

jumping

height scale

javelin throw

mattress

WINTER SPORTS

95

telpher

cable car

ski jumping

a pair of skiis

skilift

goggles

ski cap

skiing instructor

skier

track

ski-stick

snow

ski boots

ski

- Did you have skiing lessons when you were in the mountains?
- Yes, I did, but my ski boots were too big and my skiis too short and the instructor didn't have much patience. So I have decided to take up cross country skiing next year.
- When the lake freezes, the ice is so thick that we can go ice-skating on it.
- Mum and dad have bought a bobsleigh for my young brother.

- I don't want to wear a crash-helmet when I go skiing.
- But it will protect your head when you fall.
- I never fall. I've been skiing for six years now.

Santa Claus's sledge is drawn by reindeer.

bobsleigh

toboggan cap

motor-sledge

trampoline

cross-country skiing

sledge

crash-helmet

ice-hockey

hockey player

hockey stick

puck

ice

ice skating rink

ice-skates

AQUATIC SPORTS

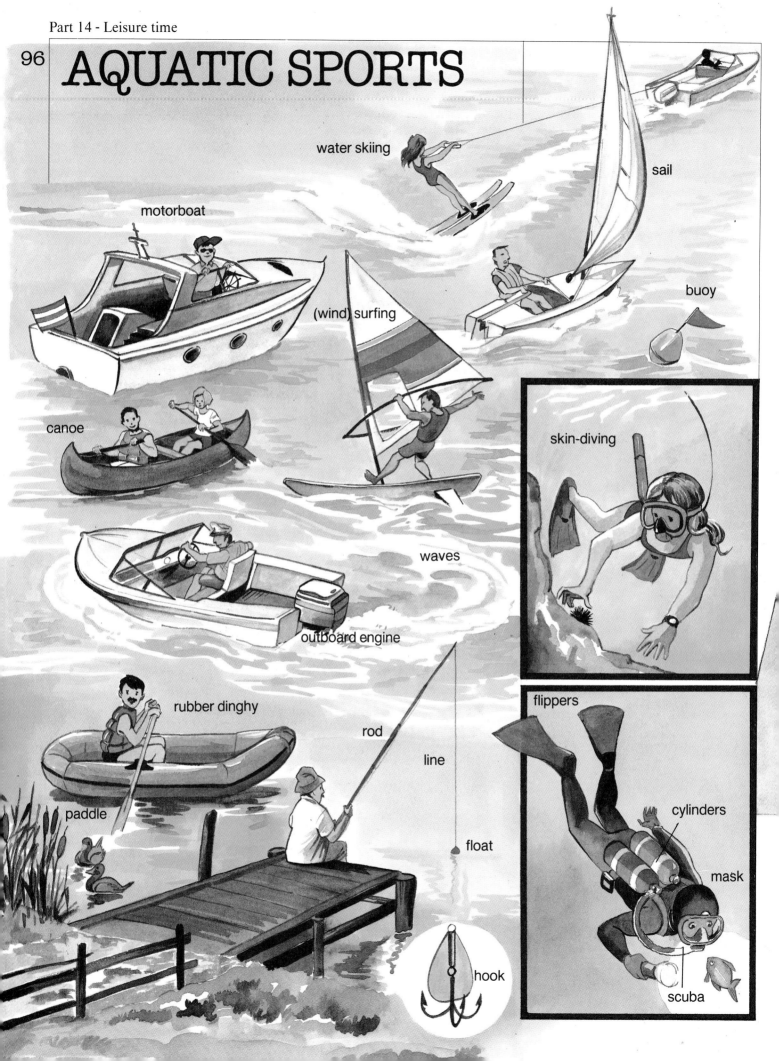

water skiing

sail

motorboat

buoy

(wind) surfing

canoe

skin-diving

waves

outboard engine

flippers

rubber dinghy

rod

line

cylinders

paddle

float

mask

hook

scuba

lifebelt

bathing hut

diving board

diving

water polo

bathing costume

swimming pool attendant

swimming

bathing cap

towel

shower

– Let's go surfing.
– No, I don't want to. The sea is too rough.

– John loves scuba-diving.
– Oh, does he go fishing?
– No, he just likes looking at the fish and the seaweed.

– I'll race you as far as that buoy.
– All right. Are you ready?
– Yes, let's go... *(splash!)*

– We've got a rubber-dinghy with a small outboard engine.

– I won't do any diving today. I've forgotten my bathing cap and I don't want to get water in my ears.

– Put your deckchair under the beach umbrella if you don't want to get sunburnt.

– John's going to have a shower, but he can't find his towel.

97 FOOTBALL

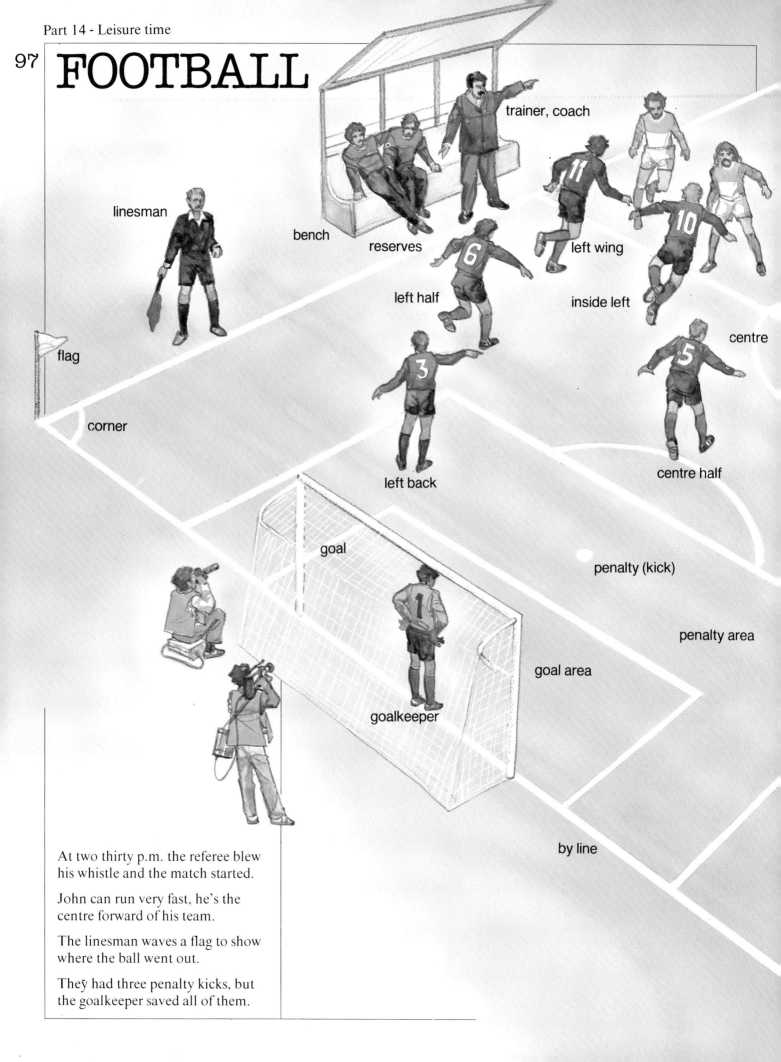

trainer, coach

linesman

bench

reserves

11

left wing

6

left half

inside left

10

centre

flag

3

5

corner

left back

centre half

goal

penalty (kick)

1

penalty area

goal area

goalkeeper

by line

At two thirty p.m. the referee blew his whistle and the match started.

John can run very fast, he's the centre forward of his team.

The linesman waves a flag to show where the ball went out.

They had three penalty kicks, but the goalkeeper saved all of them.

football

centre forward

inside right

right back

right half

referee

half-way line

right wing

touch line

linesman

supporters

THE CIRCUS

"Roll up, roll up! Buy your tickets here for our world-famous circus!"

– The band has just started playing, that means the circus has already started.

– When the ringmaster cracks his whip, the horses start dancing.

tent

band

acrobats

umbrella

tightrope walker

cage

plates

lion

tightrope

juggler

mattres

top hat

otary

ring

ringmaster

- I'm glad there's a safety net under the tightrope.
  If the tightrope walker falls, he won't hurt himself.
- When the juggler juggles plates I'm always afraid he'll break one.

- Now the lion-tamer is going to put his head into the lion's mouth.
- Where's the balloon man? I want to buy some balloons for my children.
- Look, look at that clown.
- Which one?
- The one with a big red nose.

rope-ladder

tiers of seats

safety net

audience

circus rider

balloon man

whip

lion tamer

clown

THE ORCHESTRA

– My first musical instrument was the recorder.
Now I play the piano.

– The microphone is turned off, I can't hear the singer.

– I play the violin in an orchestra.
– What's the conductor like?
– He's very good, but he's very strict.

SYMPHONIC ORCHESTRA

xylophone

pipes

organ

bassoon

flute

oboe

French horn

harp

violin

music stand

conductor

JAZZ ORCHESTRA

banjo

saxophone

percussion

microphone

singer

cornet

piano

clarinet

cymbals

bass drum

kettledrum

trombone

trumpet

tuba

viola

cello

rest

double bass

A ROCK GROUP

– I'd like to join your rock group.
– Well, if we ever need a backup singer I'll get in touch, you've got a good voice.

The microphone was too near the drummer, so the tom-toms covered the singer's voice.

amplifier

drum stick

microphone

drummer

drums

keyboard

moog synthesizer

singer

bass guitarist

The frets mark the position where you place your fingers on the guitar strings.

The moog synthesizer is named after Robert Moog, the engineer who invented it.

ELECTRIC GUITAR

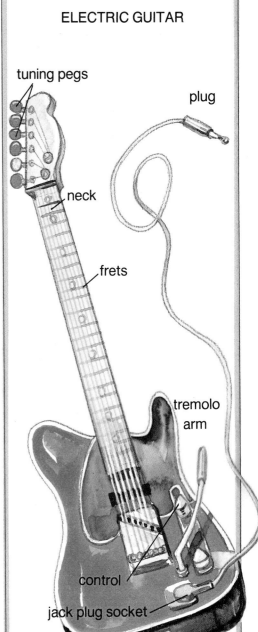

tuning pegs

plug

neck

frets

tremolo arm

control

jack plug socket

loudspeaker

backup singers

tom toms

electric piano

electric organ

lead guitarist

Loudspeakers and amplifiers are an important part of a rock group's equipment.
A sound engineer is the person who looks after the amplification of the music.

AUDIO VISUAL

– The television is not working.
– Let me see. But it can't work.
– Why not?
– You haven't plugged it in!

– Which is the volume control knob?

– Is your television aerial centralised?

– What a big screen you have!
– Well, it's a 21-inch screen.

I got a tape recorder for my birthday

video tape recorder

videotape

aerial

TV set

sport

quiz shows

cartoons

comedy

horror films

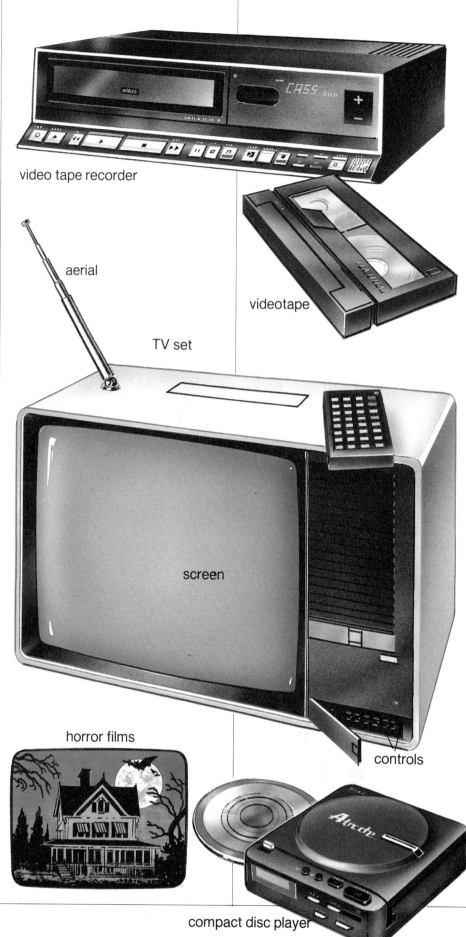

screen

controls

compact disc player

It's easy to use if you know English.
Look at the central buttons "play,
record, forward, rewind, stop"

When you are listening, the
loudspeaker should be facing you.

When I can't plug in the tape
recorder, I use batteries.

Which cassette would you like to
hear?
Let me hear that song again: press
the "rewind" button.

I've just bought a new record and
I'm dying to hear it. Where's your
record player?

The pick-up arm is very delicate
and must be handled gently.

Why don't you put the
loudspeakers in two corners of the
room?

headphones

microphone

disc-jockey

record
player

record

control desk

turn-table

pick-up arm

volume control

radio

loudspeaker

electricity socket

record

play

rewind

forward

stop/eject

flap

cassette player

spool

cassette

CINEMA

screen

safety lighting

curtain

emergency-door

audience

aisle

seats

projection room

film

projectionist

projector

playbill

ELDORADO

usherette

– I can't see the seats in this cinema.

– Let's wait for the usherette. She'll help us.

– I don't want to sit too near the screen, it's bad for my eyesight.

– The film must have been very old. It kept breaking down.

- When you go to the library, ask the librarian to show you where the children's books are.

- Silence, please! No talking in the reading room.

- Can you tell me where I can find books on the theatre, please?

- They're on the bookshelves near the window.

- Leave the books you are returning on the counter, please. I'll check them later.

bookshelf

way out

SILENCE

SCIENCE

THEATRE

HISTORY

GEOGRAPHY

librarian

CHILDREN'S BOOKS

reading room

FICTION

catalogue

picture

card-index

book

text

counter

cover

page

THEATRE

104

– I want to book two seats, please.
– In the stalls or the balcony?

The orchestra plays in the orchestra pit.

The actress was waiting nervously in the wings.
When the curtain went up she walked onto the stage.

The costumes were original, but the set was far too elaborate.

– Why are those people waiting at the stage door?
– They want to see a famous actor. Perhaps they want his autograph.

dressing room

hairdresser

wig

make-up table

boxes

wings

footlights

stalls

conductor

gallery

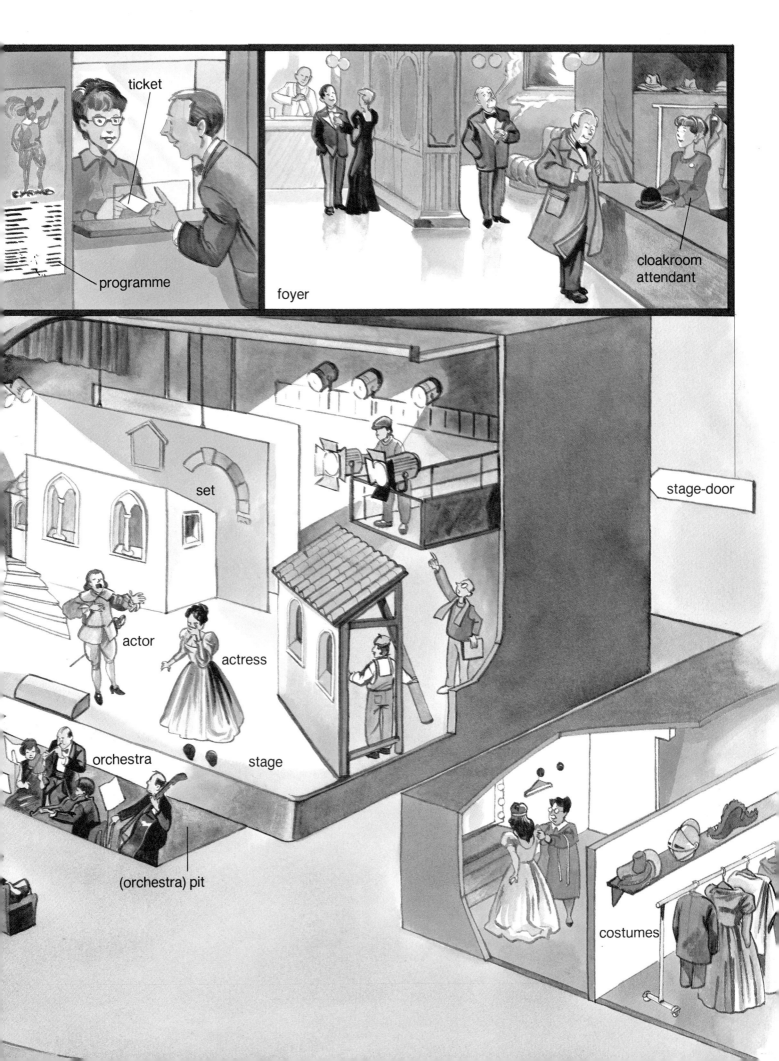

ticket

programme

foyer

cloakroom attendant

set

stage-door

actor

actress

orchestra

stage

(orchestra) pit

costumes

105 CAMPING

– Let's pitch our tent here.
– No, let's go higher up.

– We can hang the hammock up here, between these two trees.

– It's time for lunch. Look for the camp table and set it up in the shade.
Will you light the barbecue, please? Then we can cook some sausages.

– Oh, heck! The zip on my sleeping bag is broken.

fountain

mallet

barbecue

portable fridge

charcoal

camper

thermos flask

sleeping bag

storm lantern

torch

gas bottle

gas cooker

water carriers

hammock

caravan

camp bed

folding camp table

folding camp chair

tent

air mattress

rucksack

peg

AN AERIAL VIEW OF TOWN

Jane lives on the outskirts of the town.

There's a clock on the church tower.

They have built a lot of skyscrapers in the business centre.

My father works in a bank in the centre of the town.

When it's fine my grandfather sits on a bench in the park and reads the paper.

There's less traffic in the town centre since the fly-over was built.

– What causes smog?
– They say it's a combination of smoke and fog.

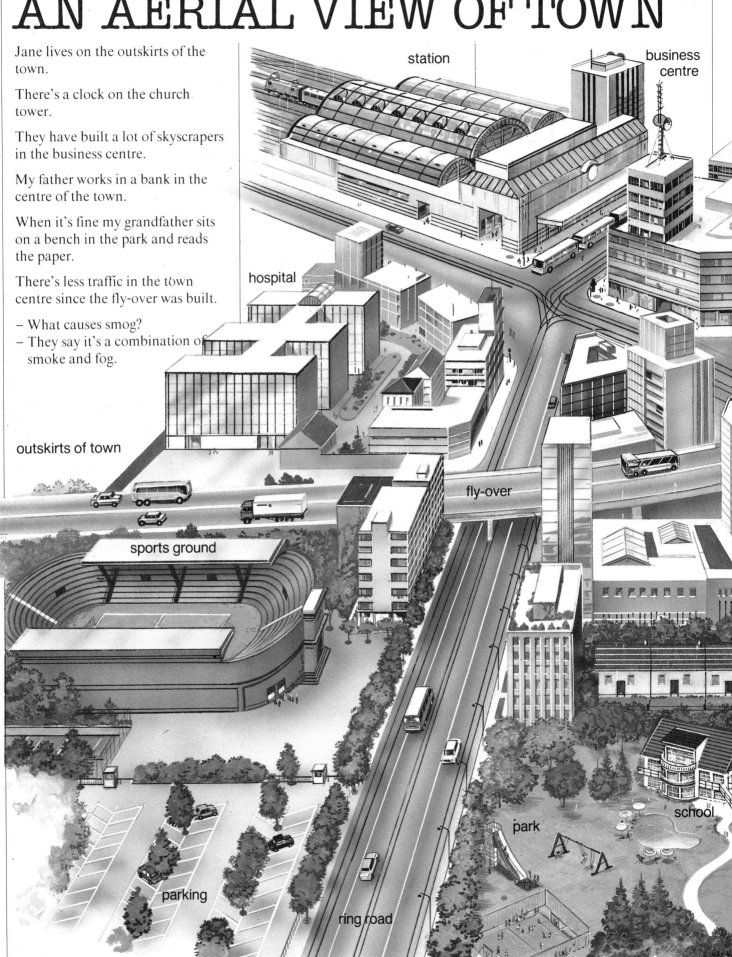

station

business centre

hospital

outskirts of town

fly-over

sports ground

park

school

parking

ring road

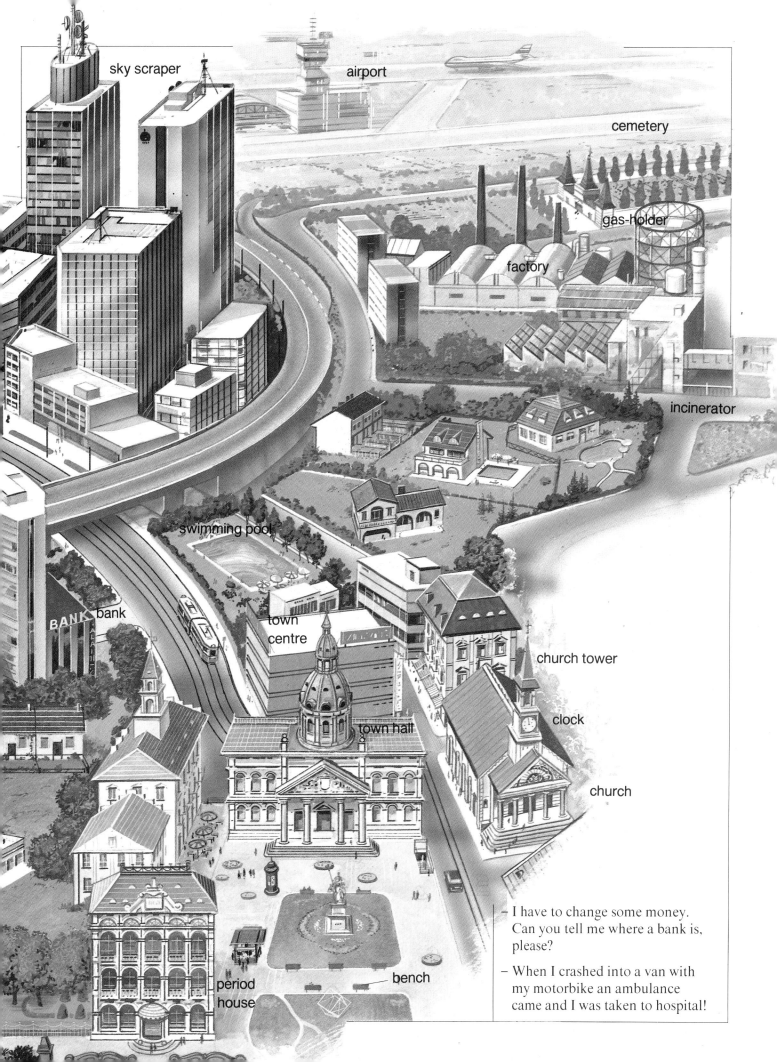

sky scraper

airport

cemetery

gas-holder

factory

incinerator

swimming pool

bank

BANK

town centre

church tower

clock

town hall

church

period house

bench

- I have to change some money. Can you tell me where a bank is, please?

- When I crashed into a van with my motorbike an ambulance came and I was taken to hospital!

107 IN THE COUNTRY

fruit-trees

silos

wheat

farmhouse

farmer spade

fields

plough tractor

church

hedge

cart

road

fisher

bridge

river

There are fruit trees and fields near the farmhouses.

The farmer ploughs the fields, then he sows the wheat.

– Look, Mr McDonald, your dog is running after the sheep.
– Don't worry. He's a sheep-dog. He's bringing them into the pen.

– What's dad doing?
– He's cutting the hedge in the garden.
– I'm thirsty. I've been working in the fields all morning.

harvester

sheepdog   shepherd

scarecrow

glasshouse

barge

fence

mill

farmyard

barn

AT THE SEASIDE

– Mum, I want to go for a swim.
– Here's your swimming costume.

– Mum, I want to build sandcastles.
– Here's your bucket and your spade.
– Thanks, mum. Do you want to build sandcastles, too?
– Thank you, darling, but I'll just sit on my deckchair in the shade of the beach umbrella.

– I'm staying at a small hotel, but my friends are camping. They have a big tent.
– When the sea is rough, the waves are big.
– Let's climb those rocks over there.

cliff

sailing boat

rocks

wave

sea

deckchair

beach bag

starfish

swimming trunks

straw hat

sandcastle

towel

suntan oil

lifebelt

sunglasses

shells

- Don't sit on those rocks. There are a lot of crabs there.

- I'm going to look for shells along the seashore.

- I want to bring this starfish home and hang it in my bedroom.
- Won't it stink?
- If I dry it in the sun, perhaps it won't smell so much.

kite

hotel

chalet

angler

boat

beach umbrella

tent

beach

swimming costume

bucket

spade

net

crab

IN THE MOUNTAINS

peak

mountain

spring

refuge

stream

hay

cable railway

field

village

woodcutter

hairpin bend

I live near a lake. My friend lives in the valley on the other side of the mountain.
The water in mountain lakes is always very cold.

In the summer we have picnics in the woods.

My brother likes climbing trees. I like walking up gentle slopes, but when the slope is steep you have to climb it. I don't like that!

You need a guide to show you the mountain pass.
That path leads to an Alpine refuge, we can have a meal there and spend the night there, too.

You can find some beautiful wild flowers in the woods in spring.

– Why are you so wet, William?
– I was so hot I stood under the waterfall for two minutes.

chain of mountains

slope

(mountain) pass

ice-axe

glacier

eagle

rock

hill

waterfall

edelweiss

wood

valley

climber

lake

hut

gentian

path

THE DEPTHS OF THE EARTH

A volcanic island is just the peak of a volcanic cone.

When volcanic ash is blown up into the air, it sometimes floats like a cloud for many miles.

A fumarole is a jet of gas that issues from the ground.

Seismic and fumarole activity can now be measured. This can help in the prediction of volcanoes.

Pompeii was buried under lava, ash and cinders when Vesuvius erupted in 79 A.D.

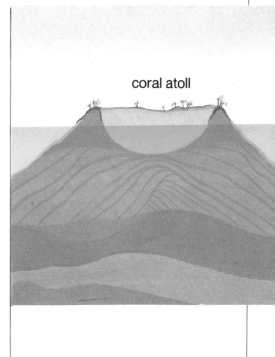

coral atoll

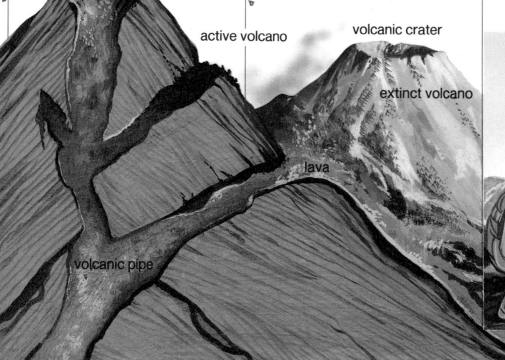

eruption

ash

lapillus

active volcano

volcanic crater

extinct volcano

lava

volcanic pipe

calcareous rock

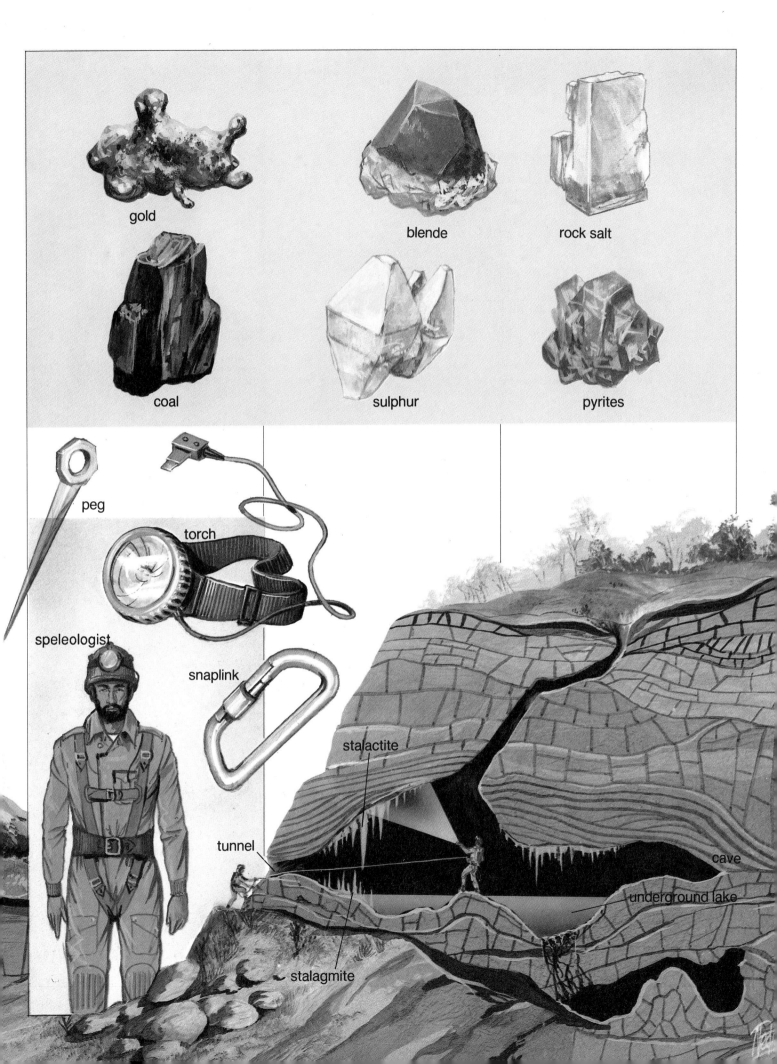

gold

blende

rock salt

coal

sulphur

pyrites

peg

torch

speleologist

snaplink

stalactite

tunnel

stalagmite

cave

underground lake

THE WORLD

111

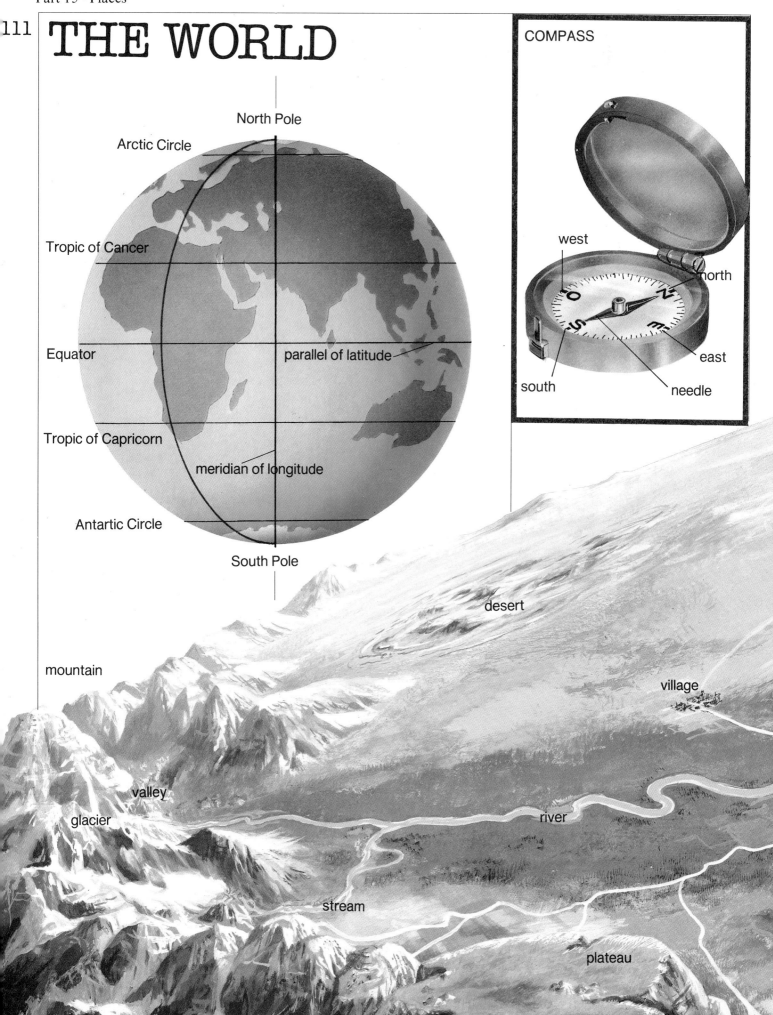

North Pole

Arctic Circle

Tropic of Cancer

Equator

parallel of latitude

Tropic of Capricorn

meridian of longitude

Antartic Circle

South Pole

COMPASS

west

north

south

needle

east

desert

village

mountain

valley

glacier

river

stream

plateau

The North Pole is in the Artic Circle.

A boy scout uses a compass to know which direction he is going in.

People go skiing in the mountains in winter.

Italy has a long and beautiful coastline.

– Mum, what's an island?
– An island is a piece of land surrounded by the sea.
– But a continent is surrounded by the sea!
– Yes, dear. But a continent is much bigger.

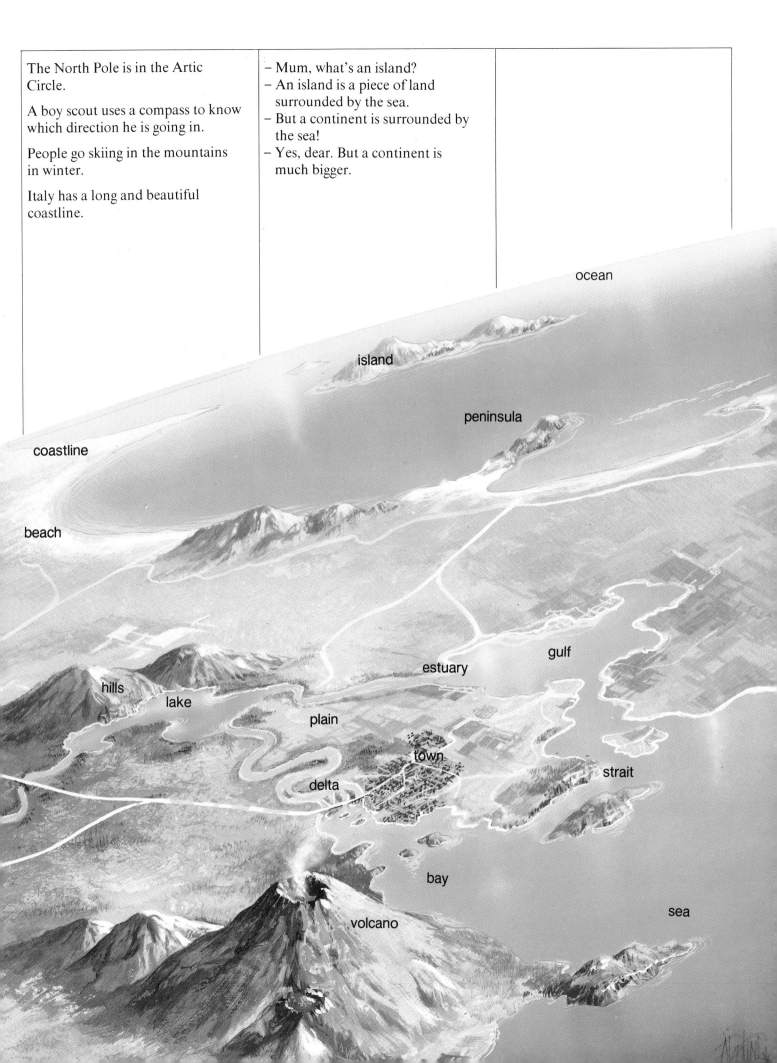

ocean

island

peninsula

coastline

beach

gulf

estuary

hills

lake

plain

town

delta

strait

bay

sea

volcano

112 EUROPE

Europe is a densely populated continent.

Many explorers like Christopher Columbus and Amerigo Vespucci, set out from Europe to discover and explore the other continents.

There are important coal and iron deposits in Europe.

The warm climate of the Mediterranean regions attracts tourists from many parts of the world.

– What do the initials "EEC" stand for?
– They stand for European Economic Community.

The Union Jack is the national flag of the United Kingdom.

Albania   Andorra   Iceland

Austria   Belgium   Italy

Bulgaria   Czechoslovakia

Denmark   Finland

France   Germany

Greece   Hungary   Liechtenstein   Luxembourg

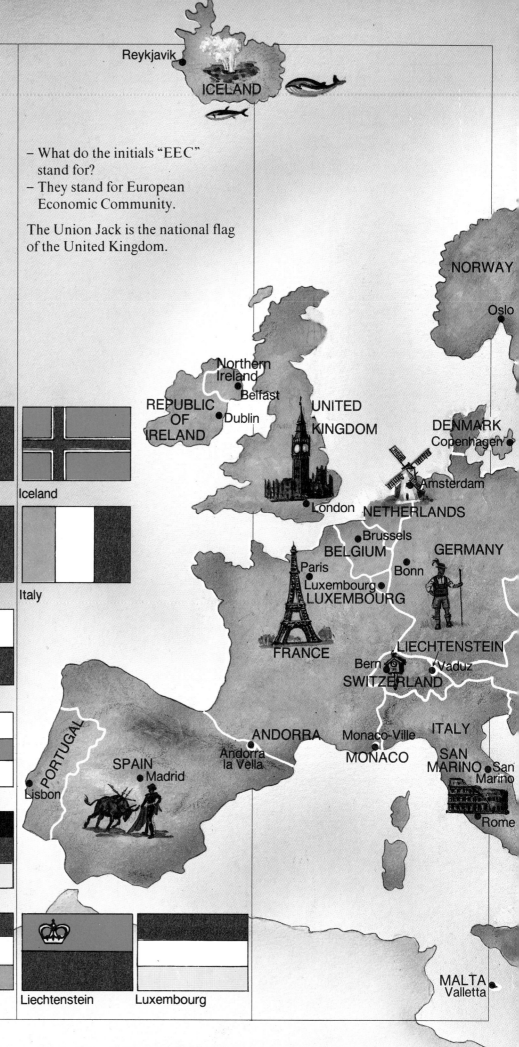

Malta

Republic of Ireland

Romania

Monaco

San Marino

Spain

Sweden

Switzerland

UNION OF SOVIET SOCIALIST REPUBLICS

Moscow ●

Norway

Turkey

U.S.S.R.

Netherlands

Portugal

United Kingdom

Yugoslavia

Poland

FINLAND

Helsinki ●

SWEDEN

Stockholm ●

Berlin

Warsaw ●

POLAND

Prague

ZECHOSLOVAKIA

enna ●

USTRIA

Budapest ●

HUNGARY

ROMANIA

Belgrade ●

YUGOSLAVIA

Bucharest ●

Sofia ●

BULGARIA

ALBANIA

Tirana ●

GREECE

Athens ●

TURKEY

cod

reindeer

forests, woods

geyser

Big Ben

(the) Eiffel Tower

wind mills

Saint Basil

glasses

watches

(the) Parthenon

(the) Coliseum

roses

space station

113 ASIA

Asia is the largest of the five continents.
It is the largest continent in the world.

The highest mountains in the world, the Himalayas, are in Asia. They are between India and China.

Agriculture is the main occupation of the people living in Asia, but Japan is certainly a highly industrialized country.

Hindu pilgrims go every year to bathe in the Ganges, for them a sacred river.

Iran

Iraq

Ankara

TURKEY

CYPRUS
Nicosia LEBANON SYRIA
Beirut
ISRAEL Damascus
Jerusalem Amman
JORDAN

Baghdad
IRAQ

Tehran

KUWAIT
Al Kuwait IRAN

AFGHANISTAN Kabul
Islamabad

PAKISTAN Delhi

Katmandu
NEPAL

BAHRAIN
Manama QATAR
Riyadh Doha Abu Dhabi
UNITED ARAB
SAUDI EMIRATES
ARABIA Muscat

OMAN

Sana
YEMEN
Aden

Afghanistan

Bangladesh

INDIA

Israel

SRI
LANK
Colombo
Male
MALDIVE

Burma   China   India   Indonesia   Japan

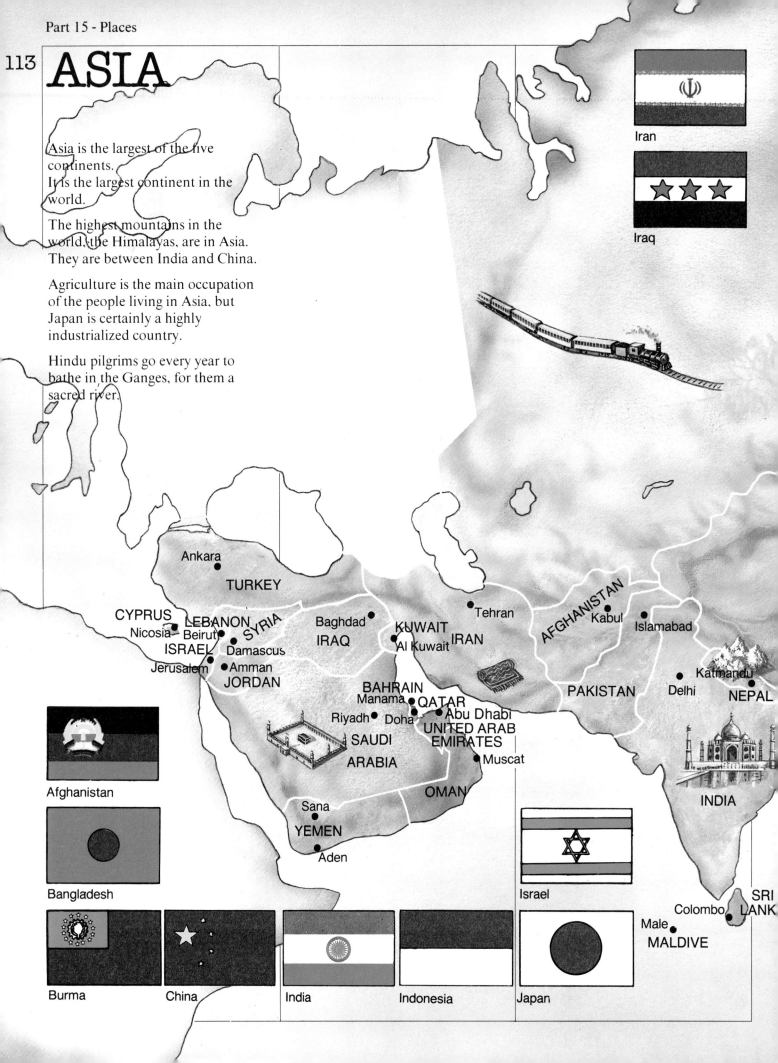

Jordan

Kampuchea

Nepal

North Korea

Laos

Malaysia

Pakistan

carpets

horses

(the) Great Wall of China

Trans-Siberian

Mount Everest

rice

electronic apparatus

Buddha

Ulan Bator

MONGOLIA

NORTH KOREA
Pyongyang
Seoul
SOUTH KOREA

Tokyo

Beijing

JAPAN

CHINA

BHUTAN
Thimpu

BANGLADESH
Dhaka

Hong Kong

Taipei
TAIWAN
HONG KONG

Hanoi

BURMA
Vientiane

Rangoon

THAILAND
Bangkok

LAOS

VIETNAM

KAMPUCHEA
Phnom Penh

Manila

PHILIPPINES

BRUNEI
Bandar Seri Begawan

Kuala Lumpur

MALAYSIA

SINGAPORE

INDONESIA
Jakarta

South Korea

Sri Lanka

Philippines

Thailand

Taiwan

Saudi Arabia

Turkey

U.S.S.R.

Syria

Vietnam

Yemen

114 AFRICA

Africa lies between the Tropic of Cancer and the Tropic of Capricorn.

Africa was called the "Dark Continent" for a long time because it was an unknown continent.

Many European countries used to have colonies in Africa.

"Sahara" means "desert" in Arabic. It is the name given to a large desert in North Africa.
In the desert, water is only found in the oases.

The river Nile runs through Egypt. The banks of the Nile form a fertile valley.

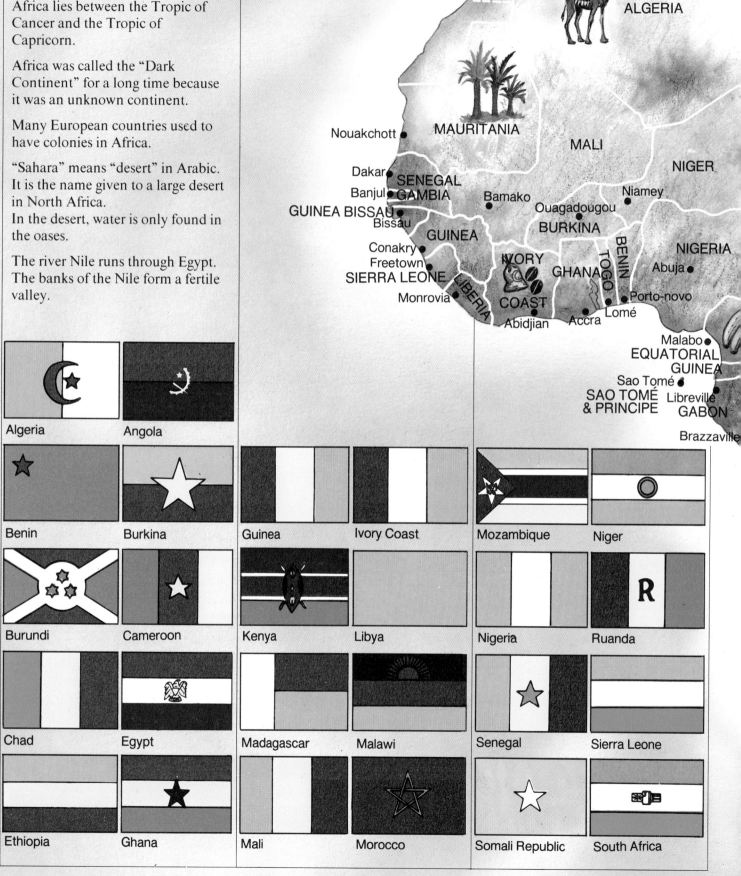

Algeria

Angola

Benin

Burkina

Guinea

Ivory Coast

Mozambique

Niger

Burundi

Cameroon

Kenya

Libya

Nigeria

Ruanda

Chad

Egypt

Madagascar

Malawi

Senegal

Sierra Leone

Ethiopia

Ghana

Mali

Morocco

Somali Republic

South Africa

Algiers
Rabat
MOROCCO
TUNISIA
ALGERIA
Nouakchott
MAURITANIA
MALI
NIGER
Dakar
SENEGAL
Banjul
GAMBIA
Bamako
Niamey
Ouagadougou
GUINEA BISSAU
Bissau
GUINEA
BURKINA
BENIN
NIGERIA
Conakry
IVORY
Abuja
Freetown
GHANA
TOGO
SIERRA LEONE
COAST
Porto-novo
Monrovia
LIBERIA
Abidjan
Accra
Lomé
Malabo
EQUATORIAL
GUINEA
Sao Tomé
SAO TOMÉ
Libreville
& PRINCIPE
GABON
Brazzaville

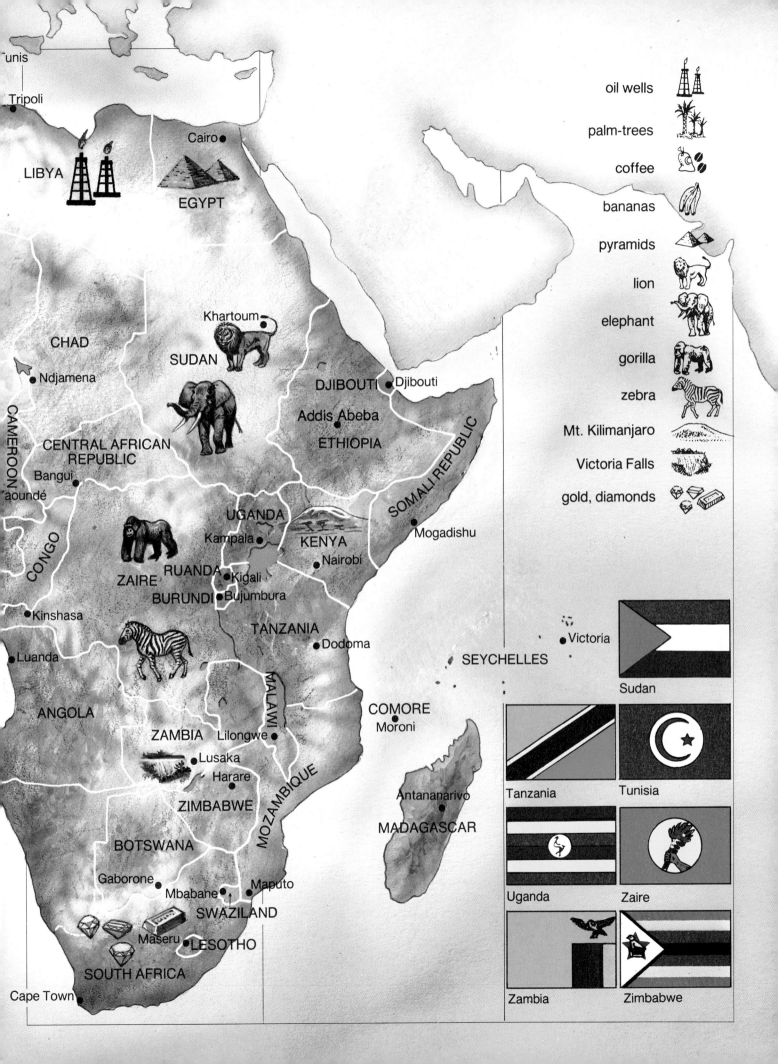

unis
Tripoli

LIBYA

Cairo

EGYPT

CHAD
Ndjamena

CENTRAL AFRICAN
REPUBLIC

CAMEROON
Bangui
aoundé

CONGO

Kinshasa

Luanda

SUDAN

Khartoum

DJIBOUTI • Djibouti

Addis Abeba

ETHIOPIA

SOMALI REPUBLIC

Mogadishu

UGANDA

Kampala

RUANDA

Kigali

KENYA

Nairobi

ZAIRE
BURUNDI • Bujumbura

TANZANIA

Dodoma

ANGOLA

MALAWI

ZAMBIA   Lilongwe

Lusaka

Harare

ZIMBABWE

MOZAMBIQUE

BOTSWANA

Gaborone

Mbabane

Maputo

SWAZILAND

Maseru • LESOTHO

SOUTH AFRICA

Cape Town

Victoria

SEYCHELLES

COMORE
Moroni

Antananarivo

MADAGASCAR

oil wells

palm-trees

coffee

bananas

pyramids

lion

elephant

gorilla

zebra

Mt. Kilimanjaro

Victoria Falls

gold, diamonds

Sudan

Tanzania   Tunisia

Uganda   Zaire

Zambia   Zimbabwe

Alaska

oil

forests

timber

seals

hunters

Golden Gate

cigars

coffee

navigation

the plumed serpent

the Statue of Liberty

Maya temple

missile

gaucho

oxen

CANADA

UNITED STATES OF AMERICA

Ottawa

Washington

MEXICO

Mexico City

Havana

CUBA

DOMINICAN
REPUBLIC

Port au Prince

Santo Domingo

Belmopan

Kingston

HAITI

GUATEMALA

BELIZE

HONDURAS

JAMAICA

Guatemala

San Salvador

Tegucigalpa

NICARAGUA

EL SALVADOR

Managua

San Jose

Panama

COSTA RICA

PANAMA

THE AMERICAN CONTINENT

– Do you know the origin of the word America?
– No, I don't. What is it?
– It comes from the name of an explorer, Amerigo Vespucci.

The Rocky Mountains run along the west coast of North America.

North America is so vast that you can find an Artic climate in the north and a sub-tropical one in the south.

You can find crops ranging from wheat to sugar and rice.

The American flag is sometimes called "Stars and Stripes".

Columbia has coasts on two oceans, the Pacific and the Atlantic.

– Can you find the Falkland Islands on the map?
– No, I can't.
– I'll help you. They are off the coast of Argentina.

– Ah, yes, now I see them. They're near Cape Horn.

– Which language do they speak in Brazil?
– They speak Portuguese.

The River Amazon is the longest river in the world. It's over 4,000 miles long.

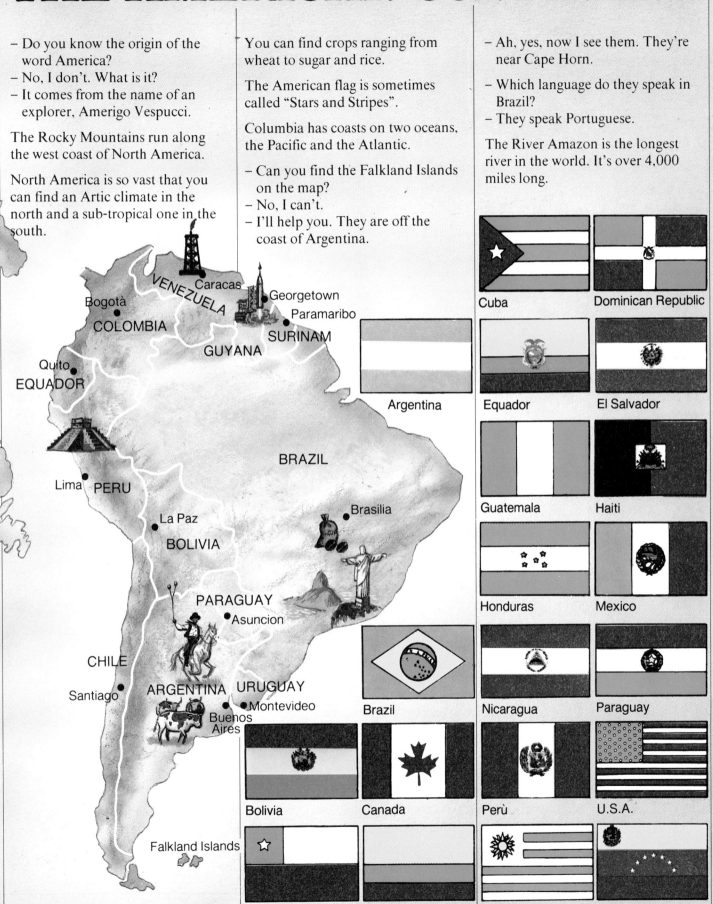

116

AUSTRALASIA

Australia is both a country and a continent.

– What is the capital of Australia?
– It's Canberra.

Australia is well-known for its sheep, but also for its kangaroos.

This continent has a long wet monsoon season and an equally long dry season with very little rain.

Koala bears, that are found in Australia, never drink anything.

There are gold mines in Australia.

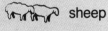 sheep

 surfboard

 kangaroo

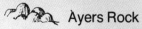 Ayers Rock

 Sydney Opera House

 kiwi

 canoe

 palm-trees; date-palms

 mask

Australia

New Zealand

Papua New Guinea

NAURU
• Valboe District

PAPUA

NEW GUINEA

Port Moresby •

SOLOMON

ISLANDS

Honiara •

• Bairiki
KIRIBATI

TUVALU
Vaiaku •

VANUATU

• Port Vila

FIJI
• Suva

NEW
CALEDONIA

Nouméa •

AUSTRALIA

Canberra •

Wellington •

NEW ZEALAND

117 STAR MAPS

Our sun belongs to the 'Milky Way' Galaxy.

On a fine night you can see about 4,000 stars shining.

The sun is the brightest star in the sky.

If you see a shooting star you will have good luck.

NORTHERN SKY

Orion, the hunter

Taurus, the bull

Gemini, the twins

Cancer, the crab

Perseus

Auriga, the wagoner

Leo, the lion

Andromeda

Pole Star, the north star

Cassiopeia

Ursa Major, the great bear

Pegasus, the winged horse

Cepheus

Ursa Minor, the little bear

Hercules

Cygnus, the swan

Corona Borealis, the northern crown

Lyra, the lyre

Milky Way

Orion is the easiest constellation to find in the sky. It is a rectangular figure.

If you find two parallel lines of stars, that's Gemini.

In Great Britain the Great Bear is sometimes called the 'Plough'.

SOUTHERN SKY

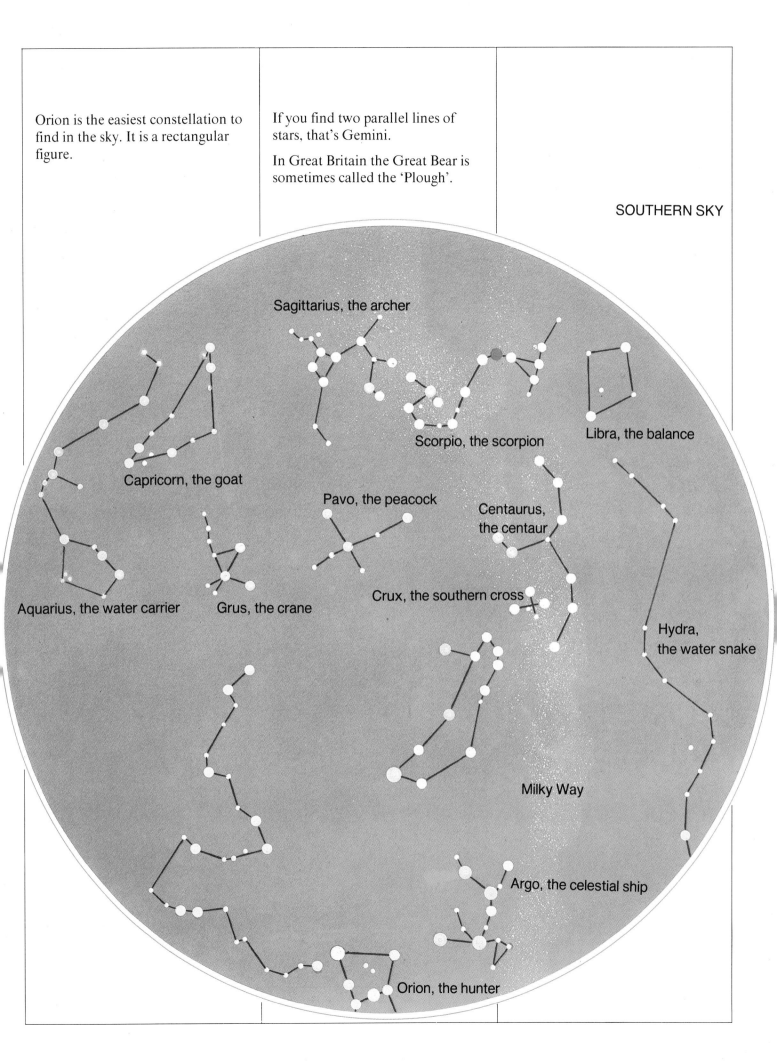

Sagittarius, the archer

Scorpio, the scorpion

Libra, the balance

Capricorn, the goat

Pavo, the peacock

Centaurus, the centaur

Aquarius, the water carrier

Grus, the crane

Crux, the southern cross

Hydra, the water snake

Milky Way

Argo, the celestial ship

Orion, the hunter

THE UNIVERSE

118

THE SOLAR SYSTEM

– The sun's shining: let's go out and play!

The weather sometimes changes, when there's a new moon.

Halley's comet won't appear again until 2062.

The moon is a planet and moves round the earth. The earth is a planet too, but it goes round the sun.

Our own sun is a burning star in the sky.

– What's a constellation, mum?
– It's a group of stars. Look: the Great Bear is a constellation.

Pluto

Neptune

asteroids

Mars

Earth

Moon

Sun   Mercury

Venus

PHASES OF THE MOON

new moon

half moon

full moon

old moon

orbit

sky

satellites

rings

Uranus

Saturn

Jupiter

star

galaxy

comet

constellation

119

QUANTITIES

– Puss-Puss-Pussy, come and drink your milk.
  Here's a big bowl of milk for you.

Pussy is playing with a ball of wool and a roll of paper.

There's gang of workmen working on the road, near a row of empty houses.

The local football team is playing very well this season. All the players have trained very hard.

What a magnificent bunch of red roses!

There are a lot of ships in a fleet.

– Do you want sugar in your tea?
– Yes, please, but not very much.
– How many lumps?
– Just one, please.

– Is there a lift in your house?
– No, there isn't. There are four flights of stairs.

a ball (of wool)

a bar (of chocolate, of soap)

a slice (of cake, of bread)

a crowd (of people)

a team (of players)

a gang (of workmen)

a heap (of stones)

a row (of houses)

a plate (of chips)

a pile (of blankets)

a loaf (of bread)

a lump (of sugar)

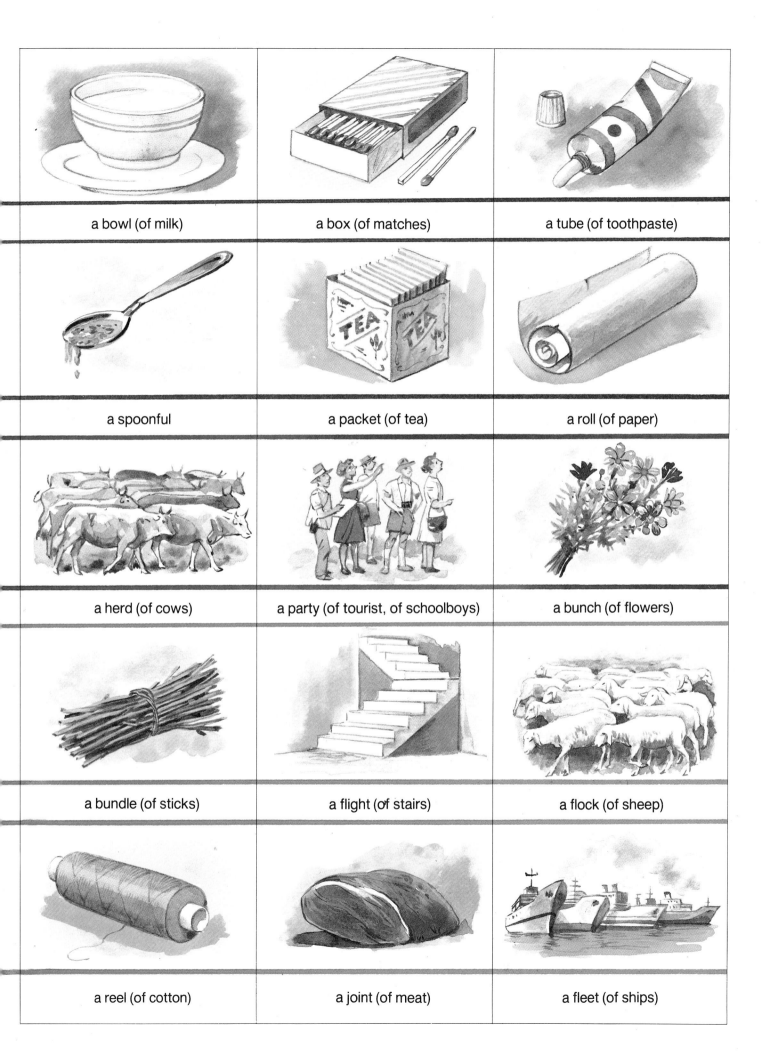

a bowl (of milk)

a box (of matches)

a tube (of toothpaste)

a spoonful

a packet (of tea)

a roll (of paper)

a herd (of cows)

a party (of tourist, of schoolboys)

a bunch (of flowers)

a bundle (of sticks)

a flight (of stairs)

a flock (of sheep)

a reel (of cotton)

a joint (of meat)

a fleet (of ships)

CONTAINERS

120

Father keeps money in a safe, but grandmother keeps her money under her mattress.

The dustbin men get up very early in the morning.
They have to empty all the dustbins before the streets are crowded with people.

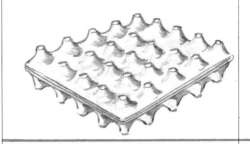

carton

briefcase

barrel

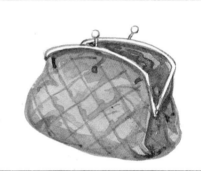

purse

paper-bag

basket

trunk

sack

carrier-bag

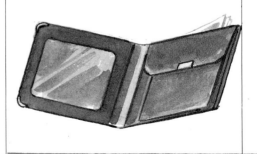

wallet

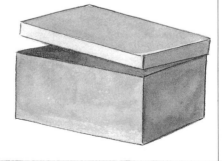

box

safe

– Where's dad?
– He's upstairs, packing his suitcase.

When scouts go camping they carry rucksacks on their backs.

dustbin

– Would you buy the paper when you go out, Monica?
– Yes, but I haven't got any money.
– Take my purse with you. It's in my bag. You'll find it on the kitchen table.

handbag

Business men always carry briefcases.

When Santa Claus has a lot of toys, he carries them in a sack.

When William was coming home last night, someone stole his wallet.

suitcase

rucksack

school-bag

(petrol) can

bottle

shopping bag

beauty case

folder

demijohn

pail, bucket

SHOPS AND SHOPKEEPERS

Fred has just gone to the butcher's to buy some meat for his dog.

If your glasses are broken you must go to the optician's to get a new pair.

I like bookshops because I like looking at books.

optician

butcher's shop

antiques

grocer's shop

ladies' hairdresser

dry cleaner

baker's shop

shoemaker

bookshop

delicatessen

barber's shop

furniture

hats shop

tailor's workroom

dressmaker

flowers

jeweller

household appliances

department store

tobacconist

clothes shop

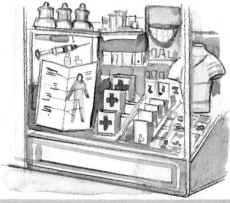

chemist's

A shoemaker will mend your shoes for you.

Are department stores more expensive than smaller shops?

The doctor has just given me a prescription, now I must go to the chemist's.

Dad has just been to the barber's. I think his hair is too short now.

122

SPORTS

Ice hockey is one of the fastest sports.

Some people attend karate classes because they want to know how to defend themselves if necessary.

tennis	ice skating	boxing
sailing	skiing	table tennis
hand ball	go-karting	rifle shooting

If you take up archery you need a bow and arrows.	My brother is so tall that he could be a basketball champion.	I like walking in the mountains, but I would be afraid to do rock climbing.
basketball	rugby	archery
swimming	rock climbing	football
ice hockey	judo	volley ball

MATERIALS

123

Ivory comes from elephants' tusks.
Bicycle tyres are made of rubber.
Gold and silver are precious metals.

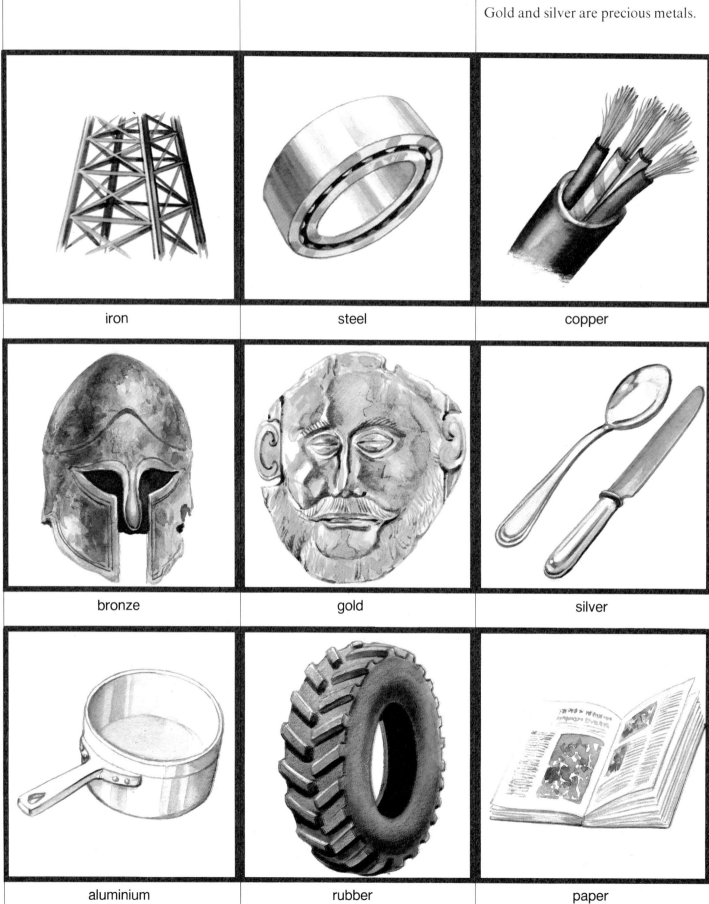

iron	steel	copper
bronze	gold	silver
aluminium	rubber	paper

This a wooden tray and this one is plastic: which do you prefer?

China teacups break very easily.

cardboard	wood	plastic
glass	ceramics	china
ivory	leather	bamboo

124 VERBS (a)

Shut the door, please; it's cold.

paint

wake up

climb

stop

throw

fly

slip

run

shut

My little sister likes *painting*, she always wants *to paint* the pictures in my school-books.	Before I go to sleep my mother always *kisses* me goodnight.	
love	drive	kiss
buy	travel	sit
go	knit	catch

124

VERBS (b)

Open your books at page ten and *read* the first paragraph, please.

pick up

laugh

wash

stay

close

break

give

think

show

If you let that carton of eggs fall, they will *break*.	I'm so happy I don't know whether *to laugh* or *to cry*.	
comb	read	fall
imagine	study	jump
push	cry	stand

124

VERBS (c)

I like *skiing* in the winter and *swimming* in the summer.

touch	ski	help
blow	lift	dance
write	smile	cheat

Don't *touch* that plate, it's hot.	Can you *help* me? I have *to learn* these irregular verbs for tomorrow.	
draw	type	pull
learn	swim	dream
visit	pay	boil

VERBS (d)

Stop *talking* and *drink* up your medicine.

I'll give you some sugar *to eat* afterwards.

walk

eat

bring

sleep

cut

watch

drink

kick

listen

Wait for me; I'll *walk* as far as the bus stop with you.	Don't *bring* it here, Paul: take it away, please.	

talk

make

look for

sell

teach

steal

put

sing

wait

125 OPPOSITES (a)

fat	slim	slow
long	short	large
dirty	clean	closed

This handkerchief is so *dirty*, I think it will never be *clean* again.

– Mum, tell us a story.
– Do you want a *sad* story or a *happy* one?

– Tell us a *sad* story with a *happy* ending.
– Well, that's not *easy*; in fact it's *difficult*, but not impossible.

fast

happy

sad

small

hot

cold

open

easy

difficult

125 # OPPOSITES (b)

Cinderella was *pretty*, but her sisters were *ugly*.

My mattress was *soft*, but the pillow was *hard*, so I didn't sleep very well.

Tom was the *last* to board the plane, but he was the *first* to get off.

soft	hard	low
full	empty	young
good	bad	pretty

high	wet	dry
old	new	old
ugly	first	last

126 PREPOSITIONS ⓐ

Where are they?

– The kittens should be *in* their basket, but the last one is getting *out of* it now.
– Where's the basket?
– It's *on* the floor *between* the table and the fireplace, *next to* the armchair.

in the basket

out of the basket

on the floor

between the table and the fireplace

next to the armchair

near the fire

- One kitten is too *near* the fire; he'll get burnt if he doesn't move.
- There's another kitten *in front of* the fire, but one is missing. Where is it?
- It's *under* that cupboard standing *against* the wall.

- Look at the white kitten trying to get *into* the bookcase!
- Another kitten is *behind* the chair.
- Where's the kitten's mother?
- She's *outside* the door. She wants to get in, can't you hear her mewing?

in front of the fire	under the cupboard	against the wall
into the bookcase	behind the chair	outside the door

PREPOSITIONS ^(b)

126

Where are they going?

These people are coming *from* the beach. They are sunburnt, tired and happy.

– Why is Johnny climbing *up* the tree?
– Because he wants the apples that are at the top.

– It was snowing when we went *into* the tunnel.
Of course when we were driving *through* the tunnel it was dark. Then, what a surprise! When we came *out* of the tunnel, the sun was shining.

(going) into the tunnel

(going) through the tunnel

(coming) out of the tunnel

(climbing) up the tree

(sliding) down the slide

(falling) off the table

(going) to the beach

(coming) from the beach

LANGUAGE GAMES
THAT'S ME

Write the number, next to the correct words:

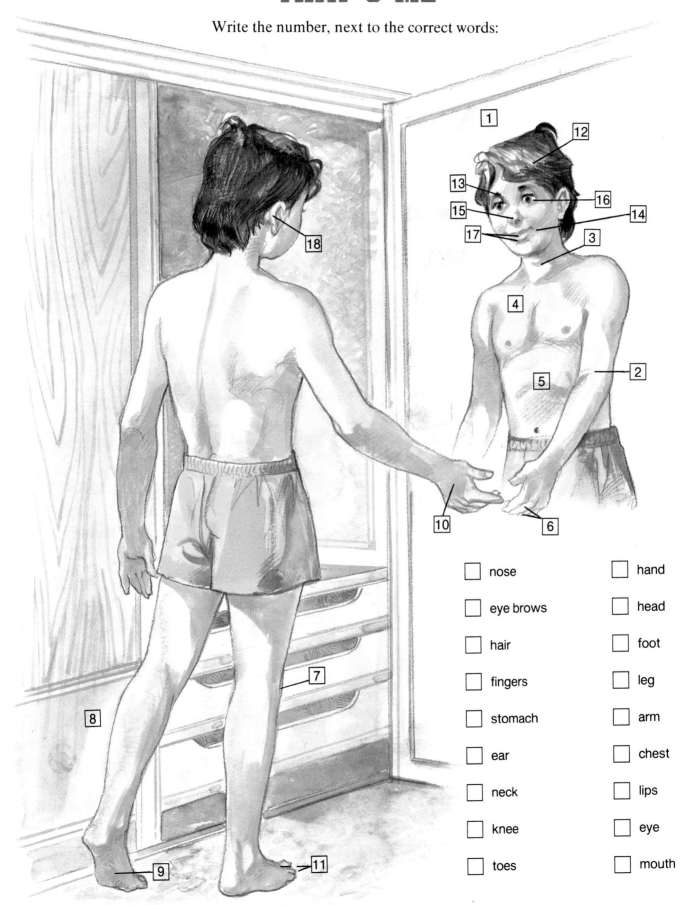

☐ nose   ☐ hand

☐ eye brows   ☐ head

☐ hair   ☐ foot

☐ fingers   ☐ leg

☐ stomach   ☐ arm

☐ ear   ☐ chest

☐ neck   ☐ lips

☐ knee   ☐ eye

☐ toes   ☐ mouth

SUMS

Do these sums and complete the puzzle:

Down

1 1 + 1 = ——————
2 5 + 5 = ——————
3 7 + 4 = ——————
5 4 + 4 = ——————
7 2 + 3 = ——————
8 5 + 1 = ——————

Across

1 10 + 13 = ——————
4 1 + 0 = ——————
6 4 + 5 = ——————
9 4 + 3 = ——————

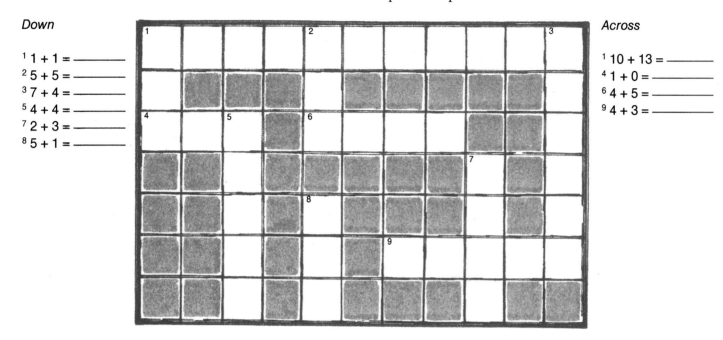

FIND THE WORDS

There are ten words hidden in the square. Can you find them?

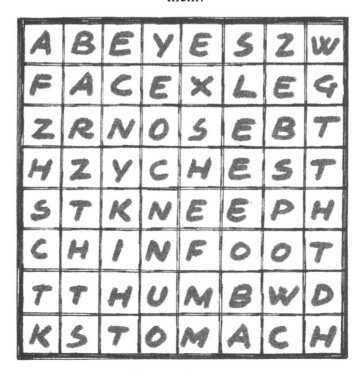

A	B	E	Y	E	S	Z	W
F	A	C	E	X	L	E	G
Z	R	N	O	S	E	B	T
H	Z	Y	C	H	E	S	T
S	T	K	N	E	E	P	H
C	H	I	N	F	O	O	T
T	T	H	U	M	B	W	D
K	S	T	O	M	A	C	H

COLOURS

All the answers are colours.

1 : _____

2 : _____

3 : _____

4 : _____

5 : _____

6 : _____

7 : _____

VERBS MAZE

Choose the correct answer and follow the line to the way out:

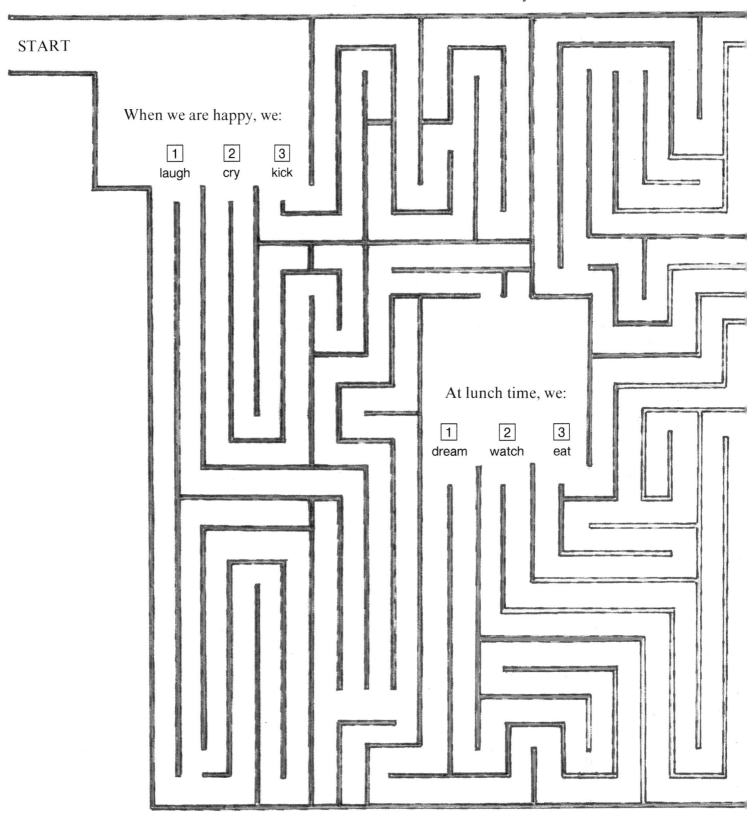

START

When we are happy, we:

1 laugh 2 cry 3 kick

At lunch time, we:

1 dream 2 watch 3 eat

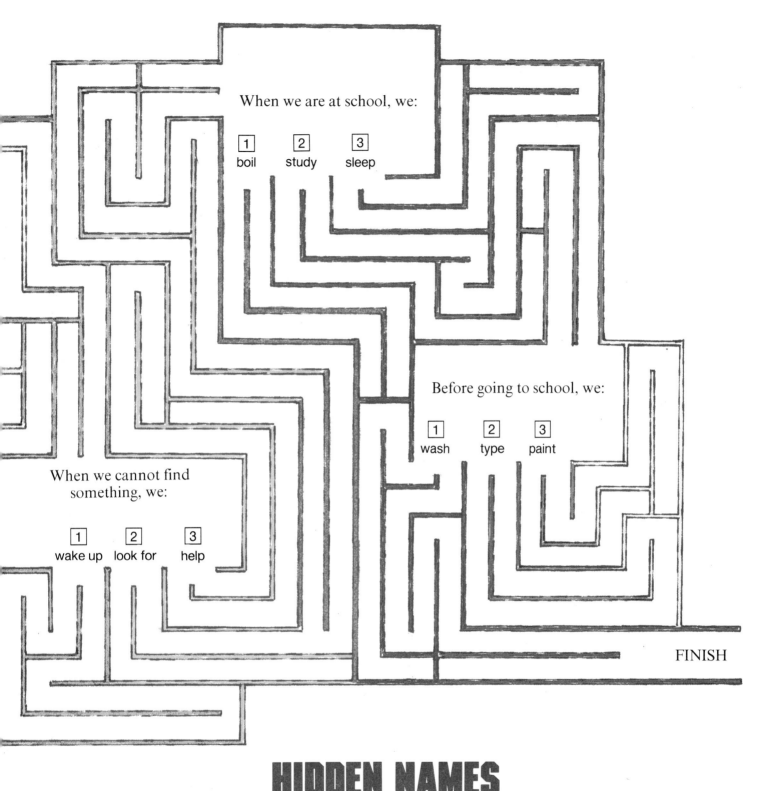

When we are at school, we:

1	2	3
boil	study	sleep

Before going to school, we:

1	2	3
wash	type	paint

When we cannot find something, we:

1	2	3
wake up	look for	help

FINISH

HIDDEN NAMES

There are boy's and girls' names hidden in these words. Can you find them?

Mar...   ...ra   ...es   Mar...   ...oline   Step...

OPPOSITES

Find the opposites and complete the crossword puzzle:

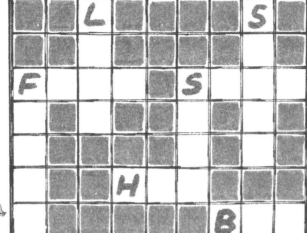

Down:

1 The opposite of first

2 The opposite of long

3 The opposite of last

4 The opposite of hard

Across:

3 The opposite of slow

4 The opposite of fast

5 The opposite of cold

6 The opposite of good

Find the opposites and complete the crossword puzzle:

Down:

3 The opposite of dry

2 The opposite of easy

5 The opposite of difficult

$2+2=4$

$\sqrt{(215)} \times \frac{a \cdot b \cdot c}{c}$

Across:

1 The opposite of happy

4 The opposite of thin

6 The opposite of fat

7 The opposite of pretty

8 The opposite of ugly

Choosing from the list, write the correct adjective under each picture:

old

new

good

bad

large

small

long

short

WHAT'S THE WEATHER LIKE TODAY?

Use the right expressions to define the weather:

it's _____   it's: _____   it's _____

it's _____   it's _____   it's _____

it's _____   it's _____   it's _____

it's _____   it's _____   it's _____

(solutions at the end of the volume)

WÖRTERBUCH ENGLISCH–DEUTSCH

A

a drop of water under a microscope: ein Tropfen Wasser unter dem Mikroskop, 28
a half: eine Hälfte, 24
a pair of compasses: Zirkel, 22
a pair of scissors: Schere, 22
a pair of skis: ein Paar Skier, 95
a quarter: ein Viertel, 24
Abidjian: Abidschan, 114
Abu Dhabi: Abu Dhabi, 113
Abuja: Abudscha, 114
accelerator: Gaspedal, 39, 40
Accra: Akkra, 114
ace of spades: Pik-As, 93
acorn: Eichel, 71
acrobats: Akrobaten, 98
Acropolis: Akropolis, 82
active volcano: aktiver Vulkan, 110
actor: Schauspieler, 59a, 104
actress: Schauspielerin, 59a, 104
add: addieren, 24
Addis Abeba: Addis Abeba, 114
address: Adresse, 49
adjustable spanner: verstellbarer Schraubenschlüssel, 63, 64
aerial: Antenne, 6, 39, 101
aerial: aus der Luft, 106
Afghanistan: Afghanistan, 113
Africa: Afrika, 114
afternoon: Nachmittag, 56
against: gegen, 126a
agora: Versammlungsplatz, 82
ahead only: nur geradeaus, 38
air hostess: Stewardess, 44
air mattress: Luftmatratze, 105
air pump: Luftpumpe, 39
air steward: Steward, 44
aircraft in loading position: Flugzeug beim Beladen auf der Rollbahn, 44
aircraft-carrier: Flugzeugträger, 55
airplane: Flugzeug, 44
airport: Flughafen, 45, 106
air-tube: Luftschlauch, 88
aisle: Gang, 102
Al Kuwait: Al Kuwait, 113
alarm clock: Wecker, 13, 56
alarm signal: Notbremse, 42
alarm siren: Alarmsirene, 52
Alaska: Alaska, 115
Albania: Albanien, 112
algebra: Algebra, 24
Algeria: Algerien, 114
Algiers: Algier, 114
Alice in Wonderland: Alice im Wunderland, 91
all vehicles prohibited: Zufahrt für Fahrzeuge aller Art verboten, 38
aluminium: Aluminium, 123
ambulance: Krankenwagen, 37, 52
ambulance men: Sanitäter, 52
American continent: Amerika, 115
Amman: Amman, 113

Amon, king of gods: Amon, König der Götter, 81
amphitheatre: Amphitheater, 82
amphora: Amphore, 80
amplifier: Verstärker, 100, 101
Amsterdam: Amsterdam, 112
anchor: Anker, 46, 47
ancient: alt, antik, 81, 82
Andorra: Andorra, 112
Andorra la Vella: Andorra la Vella, 112
Andromeda: Andromeda, 117
angle: Winkel, 24, 25
angler: Angler, 108
Angola: Angola, 114
angry: ärgerlich, 3
animal: Tier, 73, 74, 75, 76, 77, 78
Ankara: Ankara, 113
ankle: Knöchel, 1
announcer: Ansager, 59a
anorak: Windjacke, 13
Antanarivo: Antanarivo, 114
Antarctic Circle: südlicher Polarkreis, 111
antelope: Antilope, 74
antenna: Fühler, 73
anti-aircraft gun: Flugabwehrkanone, 55
antiques: Antiquitäten, 121
antiseptic plaster: Wundpflaster, 53
anti-tank gun: Panzerabwehrkanone, 55
ants: Ameisen, 73
Anubis, god of the dead: Anubis, der Totengott, 81
Apia: Apia, 116
apple: Apfel, 17
apple pie: Apfelkuchen, 16, 17
apples: Äpfel, 32
April: April, 57
apron: Vorfeld der Flughalle, 45, Schürze, 53
aquarium: Aquarium, 79
Aquarius, the water carrier: Wassermann, 117
aquatic sports: Wassersport, 96
aqueduct: Äquadukt, 83
arch: Bogen, 85
archery: Bogenschießen, 122
architect: Architekt, 59a, 85
Arctic Circle: nördlicher Polarkreis, 111
Argentina: Argentinien, 115
Argo, the celestial ship: Argo, das Schiff, 117
arithmetic, calculation by numbers: Arithmetik, 24
arm: Arm, 1
armchair: Sessel, 11, 48, 62, 126a
armour: Rüstung, 83, 84
armrest: Armlehne, 42
arrival: Ankunft, 45
arrivals and departures board: Anzeigetafel für Ankunft und Abfahrt, 43
arrow: Pfeil, 80, 87, 90
arteries: Arterien, 2
article: Artikel, 51
articulated lorry: Gelenklaster, 37
artist: Künstler, 59a, 60
asbestos suit: feuerfester Anzug, 52
ash: Asche, 110

ashtray: Aschenbecher, 11, 48
Asia: Asien, 113
assembly: Versammlung, 22
asteroids: Asteroiden, 118
Asuncion: Asuncion, 115
Athens: Athen, 82, 112
athletics: Leichtathletik, 94
attic: Dachboden, 6
aubergines: Auberginen, 32
audience: Publikum, 98, 102
audio visual: audiovisuell, 101
August: August, 57
aunt: Tante, 5
Auriga, the wagoner: Auriga, der Fuhrmann, 117
Australasia: Australien und Ozeanien, 116
Australia: Australien, 116
Austria: Österreich, 112
autumn: Herbst, 57
auxiliary turbine: Hilfstriebwerk, 44
avenue: Allee, 37
axe: Axt, 63, 80
Ayers Rock: Ayers Rock, 116

B

baby sitter: Babysitter, 59b
back: Rückseite, 25
backdoor: Hintertür, 6
back foot-rest: hintere Fußstütze, 40
backboard: Korbbrett (Basketball), 29
backgammon board: Backgammonbrett, 93
background paper: Hintergrundkarton, 68
back-pack: Rucksack, 88
backup singers: Hintergrundsänger, 100
bacon: Speck, 34
bad: schlecht, 125b
baggage claim: Gepäckausgabe, 45
Baghdad: Bagdad, 113
Bahrein: Bahrein, 113
Bairiki: Bairiki, 116
baker: Bäcker, 59a
baker's shop: Bäckerei, 33, 121
baking-pan: Backform, 7
balcony: Balkon, 14
ball: Ball, 29
ball (of wool): Knäuel (Wolle), 119
ballerina: Ballerina, 21
ballet skirt: Ballettröckchen, 21
balloon man: Ballonverkäufer, 98
Bamako: Bamako, 114
bamboo: Bambus, 123
banana: Banane, 17, 32, 114
banana (tree): Bananenstaude, 71
band: Kapelle, 98
bandage: Verband, 53
Bandar Seri Begawan: Bandar Seri Begawan, 113
Bangkok: Bangkok, 113
Bangladesh: Bangladesh, 113
Bangui: Bangui, 114

discus: Diskus (-werfen), 94
dishwasher: Geschirrspüler, 7
divide: teilen, 24
diving: Springen, 96
diving board: Sprungbrett, 96
Djibouti: Dschibuti, 114
dock: Anklagebank, 54
dock area: Anlegeplatz, 46
doctor: Arzt, 53, 59b
Dodoma: Dodoma, 114
does the ironing: bügelt, 66
does the washing: wäscht, 66
dog: Hund, 79
Doha: Doha, 113
doll: Puppe, 18, 90
doll's house: Puppenhaus, 90
dolphin: Delphin, 78
Dominica: Dominica, 115
Dominican Republic: Dominikanische
Republik, 115
domino: Domino, 21
dominoes: Dominosteine, 93
donkey: Esel, 72
donkey ears: Eselsohren, 91
door: Tür, 8, 126a
door handle: Türgriff, 8
doorman: Pförtner, 48
Doric column: dorische Säule, 82
double bass: Kontrabaß, 99
double disk brakes: Doppelscheibenbremsen, 40
double-decker bus: Doppeldeckerbus, 30
dove: Taube, 77
down: unten, 126b
downstairs: hinunter, unten, 6
dragon: Drache, 91
dragonfly: Libelle, 73, 75
drain: Kanalisation, 30
drain pipe: Regenrinne, 14
draught: Dame, 93
draughts: Dame-Spielsteine, 93
draw, drew, drawn: zeichnen, 124c
drawbridge: Ziehbrücke, 84
drawer: Schublade, 13, 69
drawing board: Zeichenbrett, 69
dream, dreamt, dreamt: träumen, 124c
dress: Kleid, 9
dresses: Kleider, 36
dressing room: Garderobe, 104
dressing table: Toilettentisch, 13
dressmaker: Schneider, 67, Damenschneider, 121
drill: Bohrer, 62, 63
drink, drank, drunk: trinken, 124d
drinks: Getränke, 31
drive, drove, driven: autofahren, 124a
driver: Autofahrer, 59a, Lokführer, 43
driving-box: Führerhaus, 42
drop: Tropfen, 28
dropper: Tropfenzähler, 28
drum: Trommel, 90, 100
drum stick: Trommelstock, 100
drummer: Trommler, 100
dry: trocken, 125b
dry cleaner: Reinigung, 121
Dublin: Dublin, 112
duck: Ente, 34, 72, 75
dummy: Schaufensterpuppe, 36
dungeon: Verlies, 84
dustbin: Mülleimer, 6, 120
duster: Wischlappen, 8, 22
dusts the furniture: staubt die Möbel
ab, 66

duty-free shop: Duty-free Shop, 45
dwarf: Zwerg, 91
dynamo: Dynamo, 41

E

eagle: Adler, 77, 109
earphones: Kopfhörer, 27
earpiece: Hörer, 49
ears: Ohren, 2
Earth: Erde, 110, 118
easel: Staffelei, 60
East: Osten, 111
Easter: Ostern, 19
Easter eggs: Ostereier, 19
easy: leicht, 125a
eat, ate, eaten: essen, 124d
edelweiss: Edelweiß, 109
edge: Kante, 25
editorial: Leitartikel, 51
editorial staff: Redaktion, 51
eel: Aal, 75, 78
eggs: Eier, 19, 31, 77
Egypt: Ägypten, 81,114
Eiffel Tower: Eiffelturm, 112
eight: acht, 23
eighteen: achtzehn, 23
eighth: achte/r, 23
eighty: achtzig, 23
El Salvador: El Salvador, 115
elastic: Gummiband, 67
elbow: Ellbogen, 1
electric engine: Elektromotor, 42
electric guitar: elektrische Gitarre, 100
electric organ: elektrische Orgel, 100
electric piano: elektrisches Klavier, 100
electric train: elektrische Eisenbahn, 18
electric trolley: Elektrowagen, 43
electric watch: elektrische Uhr, 56
electric-drill: Elektrobohrer, 63
electrician: Elektriker, 59a, 65
electricity meter: Stromzähler, 65
electricity socket: Steckdose, 101
electronic apparatus: Elektrogeräte, 113
elephant: Elefant, 74, 114
eleven: elf, 23
Elizabethan collar: elisabethanischer
Kragen, 86
elk: Elch, 76
emergency exit: Notausgang, 44
emergency lane: Standspur, 37
emergency-door: Notausgang, 102
empty: leer, 125b
enamel: Zahnschmelz, 62
end of motorway: Ende der Autobahn, 38
engine: Motor, 39, Lokomotive, 43
engine room: Maschinenraum, 47
English: englisch, 22
English stamps: englische Brief-
marken, 49
entrance: Eingang, 30, 81
entry hatch (of the space capsule): Einstiegsluke, 88
envelope: Briefumschlag, 49, 69
Equador: Ecuador, 115
Equator: Äquator, 111
Equatorial Guinea: Äquatorial-Guinea, 114
eruption (volcanic): Vulkanausbruch, 110
escalator: Rolltreppe, 36, 43

escape tower: Fluchtturm, 88
estuary: Flußmündung, 11
Ethiopia: Äthiopien, 114
Europe: Europa, 112
evening: Abend, 56
exercise-book: Schulheft, 22
exhaust-pipe: Auspuff, 39, 40
exposure meter: Belichtungsmesser, 68
extension lead: Verlängerungskabel, 65
torch: Taschenlampe, 65
extinct volcano: erloschener Vulkan, 110
eyebrows: Augenbrauen, 2
eyelashes: Wimpern, 2
eyes: Augen, 2

F

fabric department: Stoffabteilung, 36
facade: Fassade, 85
face: Gesicht, 1, Zifferblatt, 56
factory: Fabrik, 106
factory worker: Fabrikarbeiter, 59a
fairy: Fee, 91
fairy-tale: Märchen, 91
Falkland Islands: Falkland-Inseln, 115
fall, fell, fallen: fallen, 124b, 126b
false nose: Pappnase, 21
family: Familie, 5
family tree: Familienstammbaum, 5
fan: Fächer, 21
farm: Bauernhof, 72
farmer: Bauer, 59b, 107
farmhouse: Bauernhaus, 72, Bauernhof, 107
farmyard: Wirtschaftshof, Koppel, 107
fast: schnell, 125a
fat: dick, 125a
father: Vater, 5
Father Christmas: Weihnachtsmann, 18
father-in-law: Schwiegervater, 5
feathers: Federn, 77
February: Februar, 57
Federal Republic of Germany: Bundesrepublik Deutschland, 112
feeling: Tastsinn, 2
feelings: Gefühle, 3
fence: Zaun, 107
ferry-boat: Fähre, 46
festoon: Girlande, 21
feudal: feudal, 84
fibula: Sicherheitsnadel, 83
fiction: Romane, 103
field: Feld, Wiese, 73, 109
fields: Acker, 107
fifteen: fünfzehn, 23
fifth: fünfte/r, 23
fifty: fünfzig, 23
fighter plane: Kampfflugzeug, 55
Fiji: Fidschi-Inseln, 116
figs: Feigen, 32
file: Feile, 63, 64, Akte, 69
filing cabinet: Aktenordner, 69
fillet: Filet, 34
film: Film, 61, 68, 102
film cassette: Filmrolle, 68
fingerprints: Fingerabdrücke, 54
fingers: Finger, 1
Finland: Finnland, 112
fire: Feuer, 52, 80, 87, 126a

fire-brigade: Feuerwehr, 52
fire-ladder: Feuerleiter, 52
fire-engine: Motorspritze, 52
fire-escape: Notausgang, 52
fire-extinguisher: Feuerlöscher, 39, 52
fireman: Feuerwehrmann, 52, 59a
fireplace: Kamin, 11
firewood: Brennholz, 80
first: erste/r, 23, 125b
first communion: Erstkommunion, 4
first floor: erster Stock, 36
first stage: erste Stufe, 88
fish: Fisch, 16, 31
fisher: Fischer, 107
fishfood: Fischfutter, 79
fishing: Angeln, Fischfang, 89
five: fünf, 23
flag: Flagge, 43, 84, 97
flag (the Union Jack): Union Jack, englische Flagge, 47
flag dressing: Fahnenschmuck, 47
flame: Flamme, 28
flamingo: Flamingo, 75
flap: Klappe, 101
flash, flash gun: Blitzlicht, 51, 68
flash shoe: Fassung für den Blitz, 68
flashing light: Blinklicht, 46, 52
flask: Kolbenflasche, 28, Feldflasche, 87
fleet (of ships): Flotte, 119
flex: Kabel, 8
flight (of stairs): Treppe, 119
flint dagger: Steindolch, 80
flintstone: Feuerstein, 80
flippers: Flossen, 96
float: Floß, Schwimmer, 96
floating dock: Schwimmdock, 46
flock (of sheep): Schafherde, 119
flooded foredeck: geflutetes Vorderdeck, 55
floor: Boden, 126a
florist: Blumenverkäufer, 59a
flour: Mehl, 33, 35
flower: Blume, 70, 121
flourescent tube: Leuchtröhre, 65
flute: Flöte, 91, 99
fly, flew, flown: fliegen, 124a
fly a kite: einen Drachen steigen lassen, 92
flying buttress: Strebebogen, 85
fly-over: Überführung, 37, 106
foal: Fohlen, 72
foam: Schaum, 52
focus control: Scharfeinstellung, 68
focusing ring: Objektivring, 68
fog: Nebel, 58
folder: Aktendeckel, 120
folding camp chair: Klappstuhl, 105
folding camp table: Klapptisch, 105
font basin: Taufbecken, 4
foot: Fuß, 1
foot-path: Fußweg, Zugang, 6, 14
footprints: Fußstapfen, 88
foot soldier: Infanterist, 83
football: Fußball, 92, 97, 122
footballer: Fußballspieler, 59a
footlights: Rampenlichter, 104
foreign exchange: Devisen, ausländische Währungen, 50
forest: Wald, 76, 111, 112, 115
forget-me-not: Vergißmeinnicht, 70
fork: Gabel, 15, 17
forklift: Gabelstapler, 31, 46
fortifications: Befestigungen, 83

forty: vierzig, 23
forward: vorwärts, 101
foundations: Fundamente, 14
fountain: Brunnen, 105
four: vier, 23
fourteen: vierzehn, 23
fourth: vierte/r, 23
fox: Fuchs, 76
foyer: Foyer, 104
fractions: Brüche, 24
frame: Rahmen, 11, 60, Fassung, 61
France: Frankreich, 112
Freetown: Freetown, 114
freezer: Gefrierfach, Gefrierschrank, 7, 31
French: Französisch, 22
French horn: Waldhorn, 99
French loaf: Baguette, 33
French stamp: französische Briefmarke, 49
fresco: Fresko, 85
frets: Bünde, 100
Friday: Freitag, 57
fridge: Kühlschrank, 7
fried eggs and bacon: Spiegeleier mit Speck, 15
frightened: erschrocken, 3
frog: Frosch, 75
from: von, 126b
front: Vorderseite, 25
front door: Eingangstür, 14
front foot-rest: vordere Fußraste, 40
front fork: Gabel, 40
front gate: Haupttor, 84
front passenger door: vordere Beifahrertür, 44
front-wheel brake: Vorderradbremshebel, 40
frozen foods: Tiefkühlkost, 31
fruit: Obst, 31
fruit flan: Obstkuchen, 33
fruit juice: Fruchtsaft, 15, 35
fruit salad: Obstsalat, 16
fruits: Früchte, 57
fruit-tree: Obstbaum, 107
fuchsia: Fuchsie, 70
fuel (liquid oxygen): Treibstoff (flüssiger Sauerstoff), 88
full: voll, 125b
full moon: Vollmond, 118
funeral: Beerdigung, 4
funnel: Schornstein, 42, 47
fur coat: Pelzmantel, 9
furnishings: Einrichtung, 36
furniture: Möbel, 121
fuse box: Sicherungskasten, 8

G

Gabon: Gabun, 114
Gabarone: Gabarone, 114
galaxy: Galaxie, 118
gallery: Galerie, 104
Gambia: Gambia, 114
game: Spiel, 93
gang (of workmen): Gruppe (von Arbeitern), 119
garage: Garage, 6
garden: Garten, 6
gardener: Gärtner, 59a

gardening: Gartenarbeit, 89
gargoyle: Wasserspeier, 85
garlands: Girlanden, 20
garlic: Knoblauch, 32
gas bottle: Gasflasche, 105
gas cooker: Gasherd, 105
gas water heater: Gasboiler, 64
gas-holder: Gasometer, 106
gas-mask: Gasmaske, 52
gate: Tor, 14
gatehouse: Torhaus, 84
gaucho: Gaucho, 115
gear pedal: Schaltpedal, 40
gear-lever: Schalthebel, 39
Geb, god of the earth: Geb, Gott der Erde, 81
Gemini, the twins: Zwillinge, 117
generous: großzügig, 3
gentian: Enzian, 109
geography: Geographie, Erdkunde, 103
geometry: Geometrie, 24
Georgetown: Georgetown, 115
geranium: Geranie, 70
German stamp: deutsche Briefmarke, 49
geyser: Geysir, 112
Ghana: Ghana, 114
gifts: Geschenke, 20
gimlet: Vorbohrer, 63
gingerbread house: Lebkuchenhäuschen, 91
gipsy girl: Zigeunermädchen, 21
giraffe: Giraffe, 74
girdle: Gürtel, 83
girl: Mädchen, 13
give, gave, given: geben, 124b
glacier: Gletscher, 109, 111
gladiolus: Gladiole, 70
glass: Glas, 15, 16, 17, 123
glasses: Gläser, 112
glasshouse: Glashaus, 107
globe: Globus, 22
glove: Handschuh, 29
gloves: Handschuhe, 9, 36
glue: Kleber, Leim, 22, 63
gnome: Gnom, 91
go, went, gone: gehen, 124a, 126a
goal: Tor, 97
goal area: Torraum, 97
goalkeeper: Torwart, 97
goat: Ziege, 72
godfather: Pate, 4
godmother: Patin, 4
Godthab: Godthab, 115
goggles: Skibrille, 95
going to the theatre: ins Theater gehen, 89
go-karting: Go-kart-Fahren, 122
gold: Gold, 110, 114, 123
Golden Gate: Golden Gate, 115
goldfish: Goldfisch, 79
good: gut, 125b
goods train: Güterzug, 42
goose: Gans, 72
gorilla: Gorilla, 114
gown: Robe, 54
granddaughter: Enkelin, 5
grandfather: Großvater, 5
grandfather clock: Pendeluhr, 56
grandmother: Großmutter, 5
grandson: Enkel, 5
grapes: Trauben, 17, 32
grappling hooks: Enterhaken, 86
grass: Gras, 6
grass snake: Ringelnatter, 75

grasshopper: Heuschrecke, Grashüpfer, 74
Great Wall of China: Chinesische
Mauer, 113
Greece: Griechenland, 112
Greek vase: griechische Vase, 82
green: grün, 26
green beans: grüne Bohnen, 16
green grasshopper: Heuschrecke, 73
greengrocer: Gemüsehändler, 59a
Grenada: Grenada, 115
grenade: Handgranate, 55
grey: grau, 26
grip: Griff, 41
grocer: Gemischtwarenhändler, 59b
grocer's shop: Gemischtwarenhandlung,
35, 121
groceries: Gemischtwaren, 31
grove: Hain, Gehölz, 37
Grus, the crane: Grus, der Kranich, 117
guard: Zugführer, 43
guard rail: Leitplanke, 37, Reling, 47
Guatemala: Guatemala, 115
guest: Gast, 48
guide: Führer, 87
Guinea: Guinea, 114
guinea-pig: Meerschweinchen, 79
gulf: Golf, 111
gums: Zahnfleisch, 62
gun: Pistole, 21, Kanone, 55
gunpowder: Schießpulver, 86
gutter: Regenrinne, 14, Rinnstein, 30
Guyana: Guyana, 115
gymnastics: Gymnastik, Turnen, 29
gym-shoes: Turnschuhe, 12

hacksaw: Bügelsäge, 64
Hadrian's Wall: Hadrianswall, 83
hair: Haare, 2
hair brush: Haarbürste, 13
hairdresser: Friseur, Friseuse, 59a, 104
hairdrier: Fön, 10
hairpin bend: Haarnadelkurve, 109
Haiti: Haiti, 115
half: halb, 24
half chicken: halbes Huhn, 17
half moon: Halbmond, 118
half past twelve: halb eins, 12.30 Uhr, 56
half-way line: Mittellinie, 97
hall: Flur, Eingangshalle, 6, 8, 48
ham: Schinken, 34
hamburgers: Hamburger, 16
hammer: Hammer, 63
hammer throwing: Hammerwerfen, 94
hammock: Hängematte, 105
hamster: Hamster, 79
hand: Hand, 1
hand axe: Meißel, 80
hand ball: Handball, 122
handbag: Handtasche, 9, 120
handcuffs: Handschellen, 54
handkerchief: Taschentuch, 9
handlebars: Lenkstange, 40, 41
handrail: Geländer, 8
handset: Hörer, 49
hangar: Hangar, 45
Hanoi: Hanoi, 113

Hansel and Gretel: Hänsel und Gretel, 91
happy: glücklich, 3, 125a
Happy Easter: Frohe Ostern, 19
Harare: Harare, 114
harbour: Hafen, 46
hard: hart, 125b
hare: Hase, 73, 76
Harlequin: Harlekin, 21
harp: Harfe, 99
(combine) harvester: Mähmaschine, Ern-
temaschine, 107
hat: Hut, 9, 13
hatch: Luke, Klappe, 49
hat shop: Hutmacherladen, 121
Havana: Havanna, 115
hawk: Falke, 77
hay: Heu, 109
head: Kopf, 1, 73
headdress: Federschmuck, 87
headlight: Scheinwerfer, 39, 40
headphones: Kopfhörer, 101
headrest: Kopfstütze, 27
headset: Kopfhörer, 27
heap (of stones): Haufen (Steine), 119
hearing: Gehör, 2
heart: Herz, 2
hearts: Herz (Farbe im Kartenspiel), 93
heater (fire): Elektroheizofen, 65
hedge: Zaun, 6, Hecke, 107
hedgehog: Igel, 76
height: Höhe, 25
height scale: Höhenmaßstab, 94
helicopter: Hubschrauber, 44, 55
(crash) helmet: (Sturz-)helm, 40
helmet: Helm, 52, 54, 83, 84
help, helped, helped: helfen, 124c
Helsinki: Helsinki, 112
hen: Henne, 72
Hercules: Herkules, 117
herd: Herde, 87
herd (of cows): Rinderherde, 119
hermit crab: Einsiedlerkrebs, 78
heron: Reiher, 75
hexagon: Sechseck, 25
hibernation: Winterschlaf, 57
hieroglyph: Hieroglyphe, 81
high: hoch, 125b
highchair: Kinderstuhl, 20
hill: Hügel, 109, 111
hippopotamus: Nilpferd, 75
history: Geschichte, 103
hobbies: Hobbys, 89
hockey player: Hockeyspieler, 95
hockey stick: Hockeyschläger, 95
hole-punch: Locher, 69
holly: Stechpalme, 18
home: nach Hause, 22
home news: Lokalnachrichten, 51
Honduras: Honduras, 115
honey: Honig, 15, 35
Hong Kong: Hongkong, 113
Honiara: Honiara, 116
hoof, hooves: Huf, Hufe, 76
hook: Gabel, 49, Angelhaken, 96
hoop: Reifen, 29, 92
horn: Hupe, 40
hornet: Hornisse, 73
horns: Hörner, 76
horror films: Horrorfilme, 101
horse: Pferd, 29, 72, 113
horse armour: Pferderüstung, 84
horse chestnut: Roßkastanie, 71
Horus, god of Lower Egypt: Horus, Gott

von Unterägypten, 81
hose: Schlauch, 52
hospital: Krankenhaus, 38, 53, 106
hospital bed: Krankenhausbett, 53
hospital ward: Krankenstation, 53
Host: Hostie, 4
hot: heiß, 125a
hot sun: heiße Sonne, 57
hot water tap: Heißwasserhahn, 10
hotel: Hotel, 30, 48, 108
hotel bar: Hotelbar, 48
hotel bill: Hotelrechnung, 48
hour hand: Stundenzeiger, 56
hourglass (egg timer): Sanduhr (Eier-
uhr), 56
house: Haus, 6, 14
household appliances: Haushaltsgeräte, 121
household articles: Haushaltswaren, 36
housewife: Hausfrau, 66
hub: Nabe, 41
human: menschlich, 2
hundred: hundert, 23
Hungary: Ungarn, 112
hunters: Jäger, 80, 115
husband: Ehemann, 5
hut: Hütte, 80, 109
hutch: Käfig, Stall, 79
Hydra, the water snake: Hydra, die Wasserschlange, 117
hydrant: Hydrant, 52
hydrofoil: Tragflächenboot, 47
hyena: Hyäne, 74
hypotenuse: Hypotenuse, 25

ice: Eis, 58, 95
ice bucket: Eiskübel, 48
ice cream: Eiskrem, 17
ice hockey: Eishockey, 95, 122
ice skating: Schlittschuhlaufen, 122
ice skating rink: Schlittschuhbahn, 95
ice-axe: Eispickel, 109
Iceland: Island, 112
ice-skates: Schlittschuhe, 95
ignition: Zündung, 39
imagine, imagined, imagined: sich
vorstellen, 124b
in: in, im, 126a
in front of: vor, 126a
incinerator: Verbrennungsofen, 106
incisors: Schneidezähne, 62
India: Indien, 113
Indian Chief: Indianerhäuptling, 87
Indonesia: Indonesien, 113
injection: Injektion, 53
inside lane: Innenspur, 37
inside left: halblinker Stürmer, 97
inside right: halbrechter Stürmer, 97
insulating tape: Isolierband, 65
international news: Auslandsnach-
richten, 51
interview: Interview, 51
intestine: Darm, 2
into: in, in … hinein, 126a, 126b
Ionic column: ionische Säule, 82
Iran: Iran, 113
Iraq: Irak, 113

Nauru: Nauru, 116
navel: Nabel, 1
navigation: Navigation, 115
Ndjamena: Ndjamena, 114
near: nahe, 126a
neck: Hals, 1, 100
necklace: Halskette, 13
needle: Nadel, 67, 111
Nepal: Nepal, 113
nephew: Neffe, 5
Neptune: Neptun, 118
nerve: Nerv, 2, 62
nest: Nest, 77
net: Netz, 92, 108
Netherlands: Niederlande, 112
new: neu, 125b
New Caledonia: Neukaledonien, 116
new moon: Neumond, 118
new year: neues Jahr, 19
New Year's Day: Neujahr, 19
New Year's Eve: Silvester, 19
New Zealand: Neuseeland, 116
newborn baby: Neugeborenes, 4
news stand: Zeitungskiosk, 51
newsagent: Zeitungsverkäufer, 30
newspaper: Zeitung, 11
next: bei, neben, 126a
Niamey: Niamey, 114
Nicaragua: Nicaragua, 115
Nicosia: Nikosia, 113
niece: Nichte, 5
Niger: Niger, 114
Nigeria: Nigeria, 114
night: Nacht, 56
nightdress: Nachthemd, 13
nightingale: Nachtigall, 77
nine: neun, 23
nine men's morris: Mühle, 93
nine o'clock: neun Uhr, 56
nineteen: neunzehn, 23
ninth: neunte/r, 23
no cycling: Radfahren verboten, 38
no entry: Zugang verboten, 38
no overtaking: Überholverbot, 38
no through road: Sackgasse, 38
no U turns: Wendeverbot, 38
no waiting: Parkverbot, 38
North: Norden, 111
North Korea: Nordkorea, 113
North Pole: Nordpol, 111
Northern Ireland: Nordirland, 12
northern sky: nördlicher Sternenhimmel, 117
Norway: Norwegen, 112
nose: Nase, 2, 91
notepad: Notizblock, 69
(bank) notes: Banknoten, 50
notice: Bekanntmachung, 49
Nouakchott: Nouakchott, 114
nought: Null, 23
Nouméa: Nouméa, 116
November: November, 57
nozzle: Auslaßstutzen, Düse, 39, 88
nozzle of the main rocket engine:
Auslaß des Hauptraketenmotors, 88
Nuku'alofa: Nuku'alofa, 116
number-plate: Nummernschild, 39
numbers: Zahlen, 23
nurse: Krankenschwester, 53,
59a, 62
nutrition: Ernährung, 2

O

O.H.P. (Overhead projector): Overhead-Projektor, 27
oak: Eiche, 71
obelisk: Obelisk, 81
oboe: Oboe, 99
obstacle: Hindernis, 94
obstacle race (or steeplechase): Hindernisrennen, 94
occupation: Beschäftigung, 59a, 59b
ocean: Ozean, 111
October: Oktober, 57
octopus: Krake, 78
ocular: Okular, 28
odalisque: Haremsdame, 21
off: von (weg), 126b
office: Büro, 69
office work: Büroarbeit, 69
ogre: Ungeheuer, Riese, 91
oil: Öl, 16, 35, 115
oil lamp: Öllampe, 82
oil wells: Ölquellen, 114
old: alt, 125b
old moon: abnehmender Mond, 118
olive branches: Olivenzweige, 19
olives: Oliven, 32
olive-tree: Olivenbaum, 71
Oman: Oman, 113
on: auf, 126a
one: eins, 23
onions: Zwiebeln, 32
open: offen, 125a
open carriage: Abteil, 42
open-ended spanner: Maulschlüssel, 64
operator: Telefonistin, 69
opposite: Gegenteil, 125a, 125b
optician: Optiker, 59b, 61, 121
orange: Orange, 17, 32, orange (Farbe), 26
orange squash: Orangensaft, 20
orbit: Umlaufbahn, 118
orchestra: Orchester, 99, 104
order: Ordnung, 54
organ: Orgel, 99
Orion, the hunter: Orion, der Jäger, 117
Osiris, a fertility god and the giver of civilisation: Osiris, der Fruchtbarkeitsgott und Schenker der Zivilisation, 81
Oslo: Oslo, 112
ostrich: Strauß, 74
otary: Ohrenrobbe, 98
other danger: sonstige Gefahr, 38
Ottawa: Ottawa, 115
Ouagadougou: Ouagadougou, 114
out of: außerhalb, hinaus, 126a, 126b
outboard engine: Außenbordmotor, 96
outside: außen, 126a
outside lane: Außenspur, 37
outskirts of town: Vororte, 106
oven: Backofen, 7
overcoat: Mantel, 9
overhead light: Deckenlicht, 68
owl: Eule, 76, 77, 82
oxen (sing. ox): Ochsen (Ochse), 115
oxygen containers: Sauerstoffbehälter, 88
oyster: Auster, 78

P

pack of cards: Kartenspiel, 93
packet (of tea): Päckchen (Tee), 119
paddle: Paddel, 96
page: Seite, 103
pail: Eimer, 120
paint box: Farbkasten, 60
paint brushes: Pinsel, 22
paint, painted, painted: malen, 124a
painter: Maler, 60, 85
painting pictures: Bilder malen, 89
paints: Farben, 22
Pakistan: Pakistan, 113
palette: Palette, 22, 60
palla, a coloured wrap: Palla (römischer Umhang für Frauen), 83
pallet: Palette, 31
palm: Palme, 71
palm-trees: Palmen, 114, 116
pan: Pfanne, 7, Waagschale, 28
Panama: Panama, 115
panda: Panda, 76
pansy: Stiefmütterchen, 70
pantograph: Pantograph, 42
pants: Unterhosen, 12
paper: Papier, 123
paper hat: Papierhut, 20
paper lantern: Lampion, 21
paper-bag: Papiertüte, 120
paper-clip: Büroklammer, 69
Papua New Guinea: Papua-Neuguinea, 116
papyrus: Papyrus, 81
parachute: Fallschirm, 55
parachutist: Fallschirmspringer, 55
Paraguay: Paraguay, 115
parallel bars: Barren, 29
parallel lines: Parallelen, 25
parallel of latitude: Breitengrad, 111
Paramaribo: Paramaribo, 115
parcel: Paket, 49
Paris: Paris, 112
park: Park, 30, 92, 106
parking: Parkplatz, 106
parking place: Parkplatz, 38
parrot: Papagei, 77, 79
Parthenon: Parthenon, 82, 112
party (of tourist, of schoolboys): Gruppe (von Touristen, Schulkindern), 119
(mountain) pass: Paß, 109
passenger cabin: Passagierkabine, 44
passenger liner: Passagierschiff, 47
passenger train: Personenzug, 42
passengers: Passagiere, 43, 44
passion flower: Passionsblume, 70
passport: Paß, 48
passport control: Paßkontrolle, 45
pâté: Pâté, 34
path: Pfad, 109
patient: Patient, 53, 62
Pavo, the peacock: Pavo, der Pfau, 117
pawn: Bauer (Schach), 93
pay, paid, paid: zahlen, 124c
peaches: Pfirsiche, 32
peaches in sirup: eingemachte Pfirsiche, 35
peacock: Pfau, 77
peak: Gipfel, 109
peanuts: Erdnüsse, 20
pear: Birne, 17, 32

WÖRTERBUCH DEUTSCH-ENGLISCH

Bügel: bar, 61
Bügelbrett: ironing board, 8
Bügeleisen: iron, 8, 67
Bügelsäge: hacksaw, 64
bügelt: does the ironing, 66
Bühne: stage, 104
Bühneneingang: stage-door, 104
Bujumbura: Bujumbura, 114
Bukarest: Bucharest, 112
Bulgarien: Bulgaria, 114
Bullaugen: port-holes, 47
Bünde: frets, 100
Bündel (Zweige): bundle (of sticks), 119
Bundesrepublik Deutschland: Federal Republic of Germany, 112
Bungalow: bungalow, 14
Bunsenbrenner: Bunsen burner, 28
Burg: castle, 14, 84, 90
Burkina: Burkina, 114
Büro: office, 69
Büroangestellter: clerk, 49, 59a
Büroarbeit: office work, 69
Büroklammer: paper-clip, 69
Bürste: brush, 10
Burundi: Burundi, 114
Bus: bus, 43
Busch: bush, 6
Bushaltestelle: bus stop, 23, 30
Büstenhalter: bra (brassière), 9
Butter: butter, 15

C

Camper: camper, 105
Camping: camping, 89, 105
Campingliege: camp bed, 105
Canberra: Canberra, 116
Caracas: Caracas, 115
CD-Spieler: compact disc player, 101
Cello: cello, 99
Cepheus: Cepheus, 117
Chemie: chemistry, 22
Chile: Chile, 115
China: China, 113
Chinesische Mauer: Great Wall of China, 113
Chirurg: surgeon, 53
Chiton: chiton, 82
Chor: choir, 82
Clown: clown, 21, 59a, 98
Coca Cola: coca-cola, 20, Coke, 16
Cockpit: cockpit, 44
Cocktail: cocktail, 48
Colombo: Colombo, 113
Columbina: Columbine, 21
Comic: strip cartoon, 51
Comore: Comore, 114
Computer: computer, 69
Computerspiele spielen: playing computer games, 89
Conakry: Conakry, 114
Container: container, 46
Containerlaster: container lorry, 37
Containerschiff: container ship, 46
Cornflakes: cornflakes, 15
Corona Borealis, die Krone: Corona Borealis, the northern crown, 117
Costa Rica: Costa Rica, 115

Cousin: cousin, 5
Cowboy: cowboy, 21
Creme Caramel: crème caramel, 16

D

Dach: roof, 6, 14
Dachboden: attic, 6
Dachfenster: skylight, 6
Dachsparren: rafters, 14, 85
Dahlie: dahlia, 70
Dakar: Dakar, 114
Damaskus: Damascus, 113
Dame-Spielsteine: draughts, 93
Dame: dame, 21, draught, 93
Damenbekleidung: ladies' wear, 36
Damenfriseur: ladies' hairdresser, 121
Damenschneider: dressmaker, 121
Dampflokomotive: steam locomotive, 42
Dänemark: Denmark, 112
Darm: intestine, 2
Datteln: dates, 32
Dattelpalmen: date-palms, 116
Daumen: thumb, 1
Decke: blanket, 12, ceiling, 12
Deckel: cover, 103
Deckenlicht: overhead light, 68
Delikatessen: delicatessen, 121
Delphin: dolphin, 78
Delta: delta, 111
denken: think, thought, thought, 124b
Destillierkolben: still, 28
deutsche Briefmarke: German stamp, 49
Devisen, ausländische Währungen: foreign exchange, 50
Dezember: December, 18, 57
Dhaka: Dhaka, 113
Diagonale: diagonal, 25
Diamanten: diamonds, 114
Diaprojektor: slide projector, 68
Dichtungen: washers, 64
Dichtungsband: sealing tape, 64
dick: fat, 125a
Dienstag: Tuesday, 22, 57
Digitaluhr: digital watch, 56
Dinosaurier: dinosaur, 80
Dirigent: conductor, 99, 104
Discjockey: disc-jockey, 101
Diskus (-werfen): discus, 94
Distel: thistle, 70
Djakarta: Jakarta, 113
Dodoma: Dodoma, 114
Doha: Doha, 113
Dolch: dagger, 83, 86
Dominica: Dominica, 115
Dominikanische Republik: Dominican Republic, 115
Domino: domino, 21
Dominosteine: dominoes, 93
Donner: thunder, 58
Donnerstag: Thursday, 57
Doppeldeckerbus: double-decker bus, 30
Doppelscheibenbremsen: double disk brakes, 40
Dorf: village, 84, 109, 111
dorische Säule: Doric column, 82
Dorsch: cod, 112
Drache: dragon, 91
Drachen: kite, 92, 108

Drahtseil: tightrope, 98
drei: three, 23
Dreieck: triangle, 25
Dreifuß: tripod, 28, 68
Dreirad: three-wheeler, 37
dreißig: thirty, 23
Dreiwege-Kipplaster: three-way tipper, 37
dreizehn: thirteen, 23
dritte Stufe: third stage, 88
dritte/r: third, 23
drücken: push, pushed, pushed, 124b
Drucker: printer, 68
Druckhelm: pressurized helmet, 88
Dschibuti: Djibouti, 114
Dublin: Dublin, 112
Dunkelkammer: darkroom, 68
durch: through, 126b
Durchmesser: diameter, 25
Dusche: shower, 10, 64, 96
Düse: nozzle, 39, 88
Düsentriebwerk: jet turbine (engine), 44
Duty-free Shop: duty-free shop, 45
Dynamo: dynamo, 41

E

Ebene: plain, 111
Ecke: corner, 25, 97
Eckzahn: canine, 62
Ecuador: Equador, 115
Edelweiß: edelweiss, 109
egoistisch: selfish, 3
Ehefrau: wife, 5
Ehemann: husband, 5
Eibe: yew, 71
Eiche: oak, 71
Eichel: acorn, 71
Eichhörnchen: squirrel, 76
Eidechse: lizard, 73, 74
Eier: eggs, 19, 31, 77
eifersüchtig: jealous, 43
Eiffelturm: Eiffel Tower, 112
Eimer: bucket, 8, 108, 120, pail, 120
ein Paar Skier: a pair of skis, 95
ein Tropfen Wasser unter dem Mikroskop: a drop of water under a microscope, 28
ein Viertel: a quarter, 24
eine Hälfte: a half, 24
einen Drachen steigen lassen: fly a kite, 92
Einfamilienhaus: detached house, 14
Eingang: entrance, 30, 81
Eingangshalle: hall, Flur, 6, 8, 48
Eingangstür: front door, 14
eingemachte Pfirsiche: peaches in sirup, 35
Einkaufstasche: shopping bag, 120
Einrichtung: furnishings, 36
eins: one, 23
Einsiedlerkrebs: hermit crab, 78
Einstellung: focus control, 68
Einstiegsluke: entry hatch (of the space capsule), 88
Eintrittskarte: ticket, 104
einundzwanzig: twenty-one, 23
einziehbares Fahrgestell: retractable landing wheels, 44

Funkantenne: radio aerial, 88
Funkgerät: radio transmitter, 88
Fuß: foot, 1
Fußball: football, 92, 97, 122
Fußball spielen: play football, 92
Fußballspieler: footballer, 59a
Fußgänger: pedestrians, 30
Fußgängerübergang: pedestrian crossing, 30, 38
Fußstapfen: foot prints, 88
Fußweg: foot path, 6, 14

G

Gabel: fork, 15, 17, front fork, 40, hook, 49
Gabelstapler: forklift, 31, 46
Gabarone: Gabarone, 114
Gabun: Gabon, 114
Galaxie: galaxy, 118
Galerie: gallery, 104
Gambia: Gambia, 114
Gang: aisle, 102, corridor, 42, 81
Gans: goose, 72
Gänseblümchen: daisy, 70
Garage: garage, 6
Garderobe: coat rack, 8, dressing room, 104, wardrobe, 9
Garderobiere: cloakroom attendant, 104
Garnele: prawn, 78
Garten: garden, 6
Gartenarbeit: gardening, 89
Gärtner: gardener, 59a
Gasboiler: gas water heater, 64
Gasflasche: gas bottle, 105
Gasherd: gas cooker, 105
Gasmaske: gas-mask, 52
Gasometer: gas-holder, 106
Gaspedal: accelerator, 39, 40
Gast: guest, 48
Gaucho: gaucho, 115
Geb, Gott der Erde: Geb, god of the earth, 81
Gebeine, gekreuzte: crossbones, 86
geben: give, gave, given, 124b
Gebirgskette: chain of mountains, 109
Geburt: birth, 4
Geburtstagskuchen: birthday cake, 20
Geburtstagsparty: birthday party, 20
Gedanke: thought, 2
Gefangener: prisoner, 54, 84
Gefängnis: jail, 54
Gefängnis: prison, 54
gefiederte Schlange der Azteken: plumed serpent, 115
geflutetes Vorderdeck: flooded foredeck, 55
Gefrierfach, Gefrierschrank: freezer, 7, 31
Gefühle: feelings, 3
gegen: against, 126a
Gegenteil: opposite, 125a, 125b
Gegenverkehr: two-way traffic, 38
gehen: go, went, gone, 124a, 126a
gehen: walk, walked, walked, 124d
Gehirn: brain, 2
Gehölz: grove, 37
Gehör: hearing, 2
Geier: vulture, 74
Geißel: scourge, 81
Gelände: site, 14

Geländer: handrail, 8
Geländer (-pfeiler): banister, 8
gelb: yellow, 26
Geldbeutel: purse, 31, 120
Geldfach: strong-boxes, 50
Geldwechsel: currency exchange, 45
Gelenklaster: articulated lorry, 37
Gemischtwaren: groceries, 31
Gemischtwarenhändler: grocer, 59b
Gemischtwarenhandlung: grocer's shop, 35, 121
Gemüse: vegetables, 31
Gemüsehändler: greengrocer, 59a
Gemüsesuppe: vegetable soup, 1
Geographie, Erdkunde: geography, 103
Geometrie: geometry, 24
Georgetown: Georgetown, 115
Gepäck: luggage, 43
Gepäckaufbewahrung: left-luggage office, 43
Gepäckausgabe: baggage claim, 45
Gepäcknetz: luggage rack, 42
Gepäckträger: porter, 43, 48
Gepäckwagen: luggage wagon, 45
gepflasterte Straße: cobbled street, 83
Gerade: straight line, 25
Geranie: geranium, 70
Gericht: law court, 54
Geruchssinn: sense of smell, 2
Geschäft, Laden: shop, 121
Geschäfte: shops, 30
Geschäftsfrau: businesswoman, 59a
Geschäftsmann: businessman, 59a
Geschäftszentrum: business centre, 106
geschälte Tomaten: peeled tomatoes, 35
Geschenke: gifts, 20
Geschenke: presents, 18
Geschichte: history, 103
Geschirrspüler: dishwasher, 7
geschlossen: closed, 125a
Geschmackssinn: sense of taste, 2
Gesetz: law, 54
Gesicht: face, 1
Gestell: stand, 79
der gestiefelte Kater: Puss-in-Boots, 91
Getränke: drinks, 31
Getreide: cereals, 79
Gewehr: rifle, 55
Gewichte: weights, 28
Gewichtheben: weight-lifting, 29
Geysir: geyser, 112
Ghana: Ghana, 114
Giebel: pediment, 82
Gießkanne: watering-can, 6
Gipfel: peak, 109
Gips: plaster, 53
Giraffe: giraffe, 74
Girlande: festoon, 21
Girlanden: garlands, 20
Gitter: bars, 54
Gladiole: gladiolus, 70
Glas: glass, 15, 16, 17, 123
Gläser: glasses, 112
Glashaus: glasshouse, 107
Gleis: railway-line, 43
Gletscher: glacier, 109, 111
Globus: globe, 22
Glöckchen: bells, 19, 21
glücklich: happy, 3, 125a
Glückwunschkarte: birthday card, 20
Glühbirne: light bulb, 65
Gnom: gnome, 91
Go-kart-Fahren: go-karting, 122

Godthab: Godthab, 115
Gold: gold, 110, 114, 123
Golden Gate: Golden Gate, 115
Goldfisch: goldfish, 79
Golf: gulf, 111
Gorilla: gorilla, 114
Graben: moat, 84
Graben (Orchester-): (orchestra) pit, 104
Grafiken: diagrams, 69
Gras: grass, 6
Grashüpfer: grasshopper, 74
grau: grey, 26
Grenada: Grenada, 115
Griechenland: Greece, 112
griechische Vase: Greek vase, 82
Griff: grip, 41
Grille: cicada, 73
groß: large, 125a
große Trommel: bass drum, 99
Großer Bär: Ursa Major, the great bear, 117
Großmast: top mast, 47
Großmutter: grandmother, 5
Großvater: grandfather, 5
großzügig: generous, 3
grün: green, 26
grüne Bohnen: green beans, 16
string-beans, 32
Grundlinie: service line, 92
Gruppe (von Arbeitern): gang (of workmen), 119
Gruppe (von Touristen, Schulkindern): party (of tourists, of schoolboys), 119
Grus, der Kranich: Grus, the crane, 117
Guatemala: Guatemala, 115
Guinea: Guinea, 114
Gullideckel: manhole cover, 52
Gummi: rubber, 123
Gummiband: elastic, 67
Gummistiefel: wellington boots, 9, 12, 52
Gurken: cucumbers, 32
Gürtel: belt, 9, 13, girdle, 83
gut: good, 125b
Güterzug: goods train, 42
Guyana: Guyana, 115
Gymnastik, Turnen: gymnastics, 29

H

Haarbürste: hair brush, 13
Haare: hair, 2
Haarnadelkurve: hairpin bend, 109
Hackfleisch: minced meat, 34
Hadrianswall: Hadrian's Wall, 83
Hafen: harbour, 46
Hafenkran: (quayside) crane, 46
Hahn: cock, 72
Hai: shark, 78
Hain: grove, 37
Haiti: Haiti, 115
Haken: peg, 8, 105
halb eins, 12.30 Uhr: half past twelve, 56
halblinker Stürmer: inside left, 97
Halbmond: half moon, 118
halbrechter Stürmer: inside right, 97
Hals: neck, 1, 100
Halsband: collar, 79
Halskette: necklace, 13
halt/auswerfen: stop/eject, 101
halten, anhalten: stop, stopped,

stopped, 124a
Hamburger: hamburgers, 16
Hammer: hammer, 63
Hammerwerfen: hammer throwing, 94
Hamster: hamster, 79
Hand: hand, 1
Handball: hand ball, 122
Handbremse: (hand) brake, 39
Handgelenk: wrist, 1
Handgranate: grenade, 55
Handpuppe: puppet, 90
Handschellen: handcuffs, 54
Handschuh: glove, 29
Handschuhe: gloves, 9, 36
Handtasche: handbag, 9, 120
Handtuch: towel, 10, 96, 108
Handtuchstange: towel rail, 10
Handwerker: craftsmen, 85
Hang: slope, 109
Hangar: hangar, 45
Hängematte: hammock, 105
Hanoi: Hanoi, 113
Hans: Jack, 91
Hänsel und Gretel: Hansel and Gretel, 91
Harare: Harare, 114
Haremsdame: bayadère, 21, odalisque, 21
Harfe: harp, 99
Harlekin: Harlequin, 21
Harnisch: cuirass, 83, 84
hart: hard, 125b
Hase: hare, 73, 76
häßlich: ugly, 125b
Haube: cap, 53
Haufen (Steine): heap (of stones), 119
Haupthalle: main hall, 84
Haupttor: front gate, 84, main door, 85
Haus: house, 6, 14
Haus in historischem Stil: period
house, 106
Häuserzeile: row (of houses), 119
Hausfrau: housewife, 66
Haushaltsgeräte: household
appliances, 121
Haushaltswaren: household articles, 36
Haustiere: pets, 79
Haut: skin, 75, 80, 87
Hautcreme: skin cream, 9
Havanna: Havana, 115
Heck: stern, 47
Hecke: hedge, 107
Heckrotor: tail rotor, 44
Hefter: stapler, 69
Heiligabend: Christmas Eve, 18
Heimchen: cricket, 73
heiß: hot, 125a
heiße Maroni: roasted chestnuts, 57
heiße Sonne: hot sun, 57
Heißwasserhahn: hot water tap, 10
Heizkörper: radiator, 11, 12
helfen: help, helped, helped, 124c
Helm: helmet, 52, 54, 83, 84
Helm (Sturz-): (crash) helmet, 40
Helsinki: Helsinki, 112
Hemd: shirt, 9, 12
Henne: hen, 72
Herausgeber: publisher, 51
Herbst: autumn, 57
Herd: cooker, 7
Herde: herd, 87
Herkules: Hercules, 117
Herr: lord, 84
Herrenbekleidung: mens' wear, 36
Herrenschneiderei: tailor's workroom, 121

Herz (Farbe im Kartenspiel): hearts, 93
Herz: heart, 2
Heu: hay, 109
Heuschrecke: grasshopper, 74, green
grasshopper, 73
Hexe: witch, 21, 91
Hieroglyphe: hieroglyph, 81
Hilfstriebwerk: auxiliary turbine, 44
Himbeere: raspberry, 57
Himmel: sky, 58, 77, 118
hinauf: up, 126b, upstairs, 6
hinaus: out of, 126a, 126b
Hindernis: obstacle, 94
Hindernisrennen: obstacle race (or stee-
plechase), 94, steeplechase, 94
hinter: behind, 126a
hintere Einstiegstür: rear passenger
door, 44
hintere Fußstütze: back foot-rest, 40
Hintergrundkarton: background paper, 68
Hintergrundsänger: backup singers, 100
Hintertür: backdoor, 6
hinunter: downstairs, 6
Hirsch: deer, 76
Hobbys: hobbies, 89
Hobel: plane, 63
hoch: high, 125b
hochheben: lift, lifted, lifted, 124c
Hochzeit: wedding, 4
Hocker: stool, 13, 48
Hockeyschläger: hockey stick, 95
Hockeyspieler: hockey player, 95
Hof: courtyard, 84
Hofnarr: jester, 21, 84
Höhe: height, 25
Höhenmaßstab: height scale, 94
Höhle: cave, 80, 100
Höhlenforscher: speleologist, 110
Holz: wood, 123
Holzfäller: woodcutter, 109
Holzhammer: mallet, 105
Holzkohle: charcoal, 105
Holzkohlengrill: barbecue, 105
Holzstoß: bundles of sticks, 87
Honduras: Honduras, 115
Hongkong: Hong Kong, 113
Honiara: Honiara, 116
Honig: honey, 15, 35
Hörer: earpiece, 49, handset, 49, receiver,
8, 49
Hörnchen: croissant, 15
Hörner: horns, 76
Hornisse: hornet, 73
Horrorfilme: horror films, 101
Horus, Gott von Unterägypten: Horus, god
of Lower Egypt, 81
Hosen: trousers, 9, 12
Hostie: Host, 4
Hotel: hotel, 30, 48, 108
Hotelbar: hotel bar, 48
Hotelrechnung: hotel bill, 48
hübsch: pretty, 125b
Hubschrauber: helicopter, 44, 55
Huf, Hufe: hoof, hooves, 76
Hügel: hill, 109, 111
Huhn: chicken, 34
Hühner auf dem Bratspieß: chickens,
roasting on the spit, 31
Hummer: lobster, 78
Hund: dog, 79
Hundehütte: kennel, 79
Hundeleine: lead, 79
hundert: hundred, 23

Hupe: horn, 40
Hupe: klaxon, 40
Hut: hat, 9, 13
Hutmacherladen: hat shop, 121
Hütte: chalet, 108, hut, 80, 109
Hyäne: hyena, 74
Hydra, die Wasserschlange: Hydra, the
water snake, 117
Hydrant: hydrant, 52
Hypotenuse: hypotenuse, 25

I

Igel: hedgehog, 76
in, im: in, 126a
in, in … hinein: into, 126a, 126b
Indianer: Red Indians, 87
Indianerfrau: squaw, 87
Indianerhäuptling: Indian Chief, 87
Indianerzelt: tepee, 87
Indien: India, 113
Indonesien: Indonesia, 113
Infanterist: foot soldier, 83
Injektion: injection, 53
Innenspur: inside lane, 37
ins Theater gehen: going to the theatre, 89
Insel: island, 111
Interview: interview, 51
ionische Säule: Ionic column, 82
Irak: Iraq, 113
Iran: Iran, 113
Isis, Königin der Götter: Isis, queen of the
gods, 81
Islamabad: Islamabad, 113
Island: Iceland, 112
Isolierband: insulating tape, 65
Israel: Israel, 113
Italien: Italy, 112

J

Jacke: jacket, 9, 12, 36
Jäger: hunters, 80, 115
Jaguar: jaguar, 76
Jahreszeit: season, 57
Jamaika: Jamaica, 115
Januar: January, 57
Japan: Japan, 113
Jazz-Orchester: jazz orchestra, 99
Jeans: jeans, 12
Jeep: jeep, 55
Jemen: Yemen, 113
Jerusalem: Jerusalem, 113
Jogging: jogging, 89
Joghurt: yoghurt, 15
Joker: joker, 93
Jongleur: juggler, 98
Jordanien: Jordan, 113
Journalismus: journalism, 51
Journalist: journalist, 59b
Judo: judo, 122
Judoka: judoka, 29
Jugoslawien: Yugoslavia, 112
Juli: July, 57
jung: young, 125b

Nouakchott: Nouakchott, 114
Nouméa: Nouméa, 116
November: November, 57
Nuku'alofa: Nuku'alofa, 116
Null: nought, 23
Null: zero, 23
Nummernschild: number-plate, 39
nur geradeaus: ahead only, 38
Nutzholz: timber, 42, 115

O

Obelisk: obelisk, 81
oben: upstairs, 6
Oberseite: top, 25
Objektivring: focusing ring, 68
Objektträger: slides, 28
Oboe: oboe, 99
Obst: fruit, 31
Obstbaum: fruit-tree, 107
Obstkorb: basket of fruits, 17
Obstkuchen: fruit flan, 33
Obstsalat: fruit salad, 16
Ochsen (Ochse): oxen
(sing. ox), 115
offen: open, 125a
Ohren: ears, 2
Ohrenrobbe: otary, 98
Oktober: October, 57
Okular: ocular, 28
Öl: oil, 16, 35, 115
Ölfarbentuben: tubes of
oil paint, 60
Oliven: olives, 32
Olivenbaum: olive-tree, 71
Olivenzweige: olive branches, 19
Öllampe: oil lamp, 82
Ölquellen: oil wells, 114
Ölsardinen: sardines in oil, 35
Öltanker: tanker, 46
Oman: Oman, 113
Onkel: uncle, 5
Oper von Sydney: Sydney Opera
House, 116
Optiker: optician, 59b, 61, 121
Orange: orange, 17, 32
orange (Farbe): orange, 26
Orangenmarmelade: marmalade, 15
Orangensaft: orange squash, 20
Orchester: orchestra, 99, 104
Ordnung: order, 54
Orgel: organ, 99
Orgelpfeifen: pipes, 99
Orion, der Jäger: Orion, the hunter, 117
Osiris, der Fruchtbarkeitsgott und
Schenker der Zivilisation: Osiris, a fertility
god and the giver of
civilisation, 81†
Oslo: Oslo, 112
Osten: East, 111
Osterblume: daffodil, 57, 70
Ostereier: Easter eggs, 19
Ostern: Easter, 19
Österreich: Austria, 112
Ottawa: Ottawa, 115
Ouagadougou: Ouagadougou, 114
Overhead-Projektor: O.H.P. (Overhead
projector), 27
Ozean: ocean, 111

P

Päckchen (Tee): packet (of tea), 119
Paddel: paddle, 96
Paket: parcel, 49
Pakistan: Pakistan, 113
Palette: palette, 22, 60, pallet, 31
Palla (römischer Umhang für Frauen):
palla, a coloured wrap, 83
Palme: palm, 71
Palmen: palm-trees, 114, 116
Panama: Panama, 115
Panda: panda, 76
Pantoffel: slippers, 12, 13
Pantograph: pantograph, 42
Panzer: tank, 55
Panzerabwehrkanone: anti-tank gun, 55
Panzerkammer: strong room, 50
Papagei: parrot, 77, 79
Papier: paper, 123
Papierhut: paper hat, 20
Papierkorb: waste-paper basket, 12, 69,
waste-paper bin, 22
Papierrolle: roll (of paper), 119
Papiertüte: paper-bag, 120
Pappel: poplar, 71
Pappnase: false nose, 21
Papua-Neuguinea: Papua New
Guinea, 116
Papyrus: papyrus, 81
Paraguay: Paraguay, 115
Parallelen: parallel lines, 25
Paramaribo: Paramaribo, 115
Parfüm: perfume, 13
Paris: Paris, 112
Park: park, 30, 92, 106
Parkettsitze: stalls, 104
Parkplatz: car park, 45, parking, 106, park-
ing place, 106
Parkverbot: no waiting, 38
Parthenon: Parthenon, 82, 112
Passagiere: passengers, 43, 44
Passagierkabine: passenger cabin, 44
Passagierschiff: passenger liner, 47
Passionsblume: passion flower, 70
Paß: (mountain) pass, 109, passport, 48
Paßkontrolle: passport control, 45
Pate: godfather, 4
Pâté: pâté, 34
Patient: patient, 53, 62
Patin: godmother, 4
Patrone: cartridge, 55
Pause: break, 22
Pavo, der Pfau: Pavo, the peacock, 117
Pedal: pedal, 41
Pegasus, das geflügelte Pferd: Pegasus,
the winged horse, 117
Peitsche: whip, 98
Peking: Beijing, 113
Pelzmantel: fur coat, 9
Pendel: pendulum, 56
Penduluhr: grandfather clock, 56
Penny: penny, 50
Peplos: peplos, 82
Periskop: periscope, 46, 55
Perseus: Perseus, 117
Personenzug: passenger train, 42
Peru: Perù, 115
Perücke: wig, 54, 104
Pfad: path, 109
Pfahlbauten: pile-dwelling, 80

Pfanne: pan, 7
Pfau: peacock, 77
Pfeffer: pepper, 15, 16
Pfefferschoten: peppers, 32
Pfeife: whistle, 90
Pfeil: arrow, 80, 87, 90
Pferd: horse, 29, 72, 113
Pferderüstung: horse armour, 84
Pfirsiche: peaches, 32
Pflanze: plant, 6, 11, 70
Pflug: plough, 107
Pförtner: doorman, 48
Pfropfen: stopper, 28
Pfund: pound, 50
Pfütze: puddle, 58
Pharao: pharaoh, 81
Philippinen: Philippines, 113
Phnom Penh: Phnom Penh, 113
Pianist: pianist, 59b
Pier: pier, 46
Pierrot: Pierrot, 21
Pik: spades, 93
Pik-As: ace of spades, 93
Pilot: pilot, 44, 59b
Pilze: mushrooms, 32, 57, 91
Pinguin: penguin, 78
Pinie: pine, 71
Pinocchio: Pinocchio, 91
Pinsel: brush, 60
Pinsel: paint brushes, 22
Pionier: pioneer, 87
Pirat: pirate, 21, 86
Piratenflagge: pirate flag, 86
Pistole: gun, 21
Pistole: pistol, 55, 86
Plan, Karte: map, 22, 117, 86
Plan: plan, 85
Plastik: plastic, 123
Platane: plane tree, 71
Plateau, Hochebene: plateau, 111
Plattenspieler: record player, 101
Plattenteller: turn-table, 101
Platz: square, 30
Platzanweiserin: usherette, 102
Plum Pudding: plum pudding, 18
Plüschtier: cuddly toy, 90
Plüschtier: soft toy, 90
Pluto: Pluto, 118
Polarstern, der Nordstern: Pole Star, the
North Star, 117
Polen: Poland, 112
Polizeiauto: police-car, 54
Polizeihund: police-dog, 54
Polizeiinspektor: police inspector, 54
Polizeiwache: police station, 54
Polizist: policeman, 54, 59b
Polizistin: policewomen, 59b
Poller: bollard, 46
polnische Briefmarke: Polish stamp, 49
Pommes frites: chips, 16
Popcorn: popcorn, 20
Porridge: porridge, 15
Port au Prince: Port au Prince, 115
Port Louis: Port Louis, 114
Port Moresby: Port Moresby, 116
Port Vila: Port Vila, 116
Portier: porter, 59b
Porto-novo: Porto-novo, 114
Portugal: Portugal, 112
Porzellan: china, 123
Posaune: trombone, 99
Postamt: post office, 30, 49
Poster: poster, 22

Türgriff: door handle, 8
Türkette: lock and chain, 8
Turm: tower, 84
Turm (Schach): castle, 93
Türmchen: turret, 55
Turnier: tournament, 84
Turnschuhe: gym-shoes, 12, plimsolls, 12
Tuvalu: Tuvalu, 116

U

U-Bahnstation: underground station, 43
U-Boot: submarine, 46, 55
Überführung: fly-over, 37, 106
Überholverbot: no overtaking, 38
Übersetzung: translation, 27
Uganda: Uganda, 114
Uhr: clock, 11, 56, 106
Uhren: watches, 56, 112
Uhrmacher: watchmaker, 56
Ulan Bator: Ulan Bator, 113
Umfang: circumference, 25
Umkleidekabine: changing booth, 36,
bathing hut, 96
Umlaufbahn: orbit, 118
unbeschrankter Bahnübergang: level
crossing without barrier ahead, 38
Ungarn: Hungary, 112
Ungeheuer: ogre, 91
Uniform: uniform, 54
Union der Sozialistischen Sowjetrepubli-
ken: Union of Soviet Socialist
Republics, 112
Union Jack, englische Flagge: flag (the
Union Jack), 47
Universum: universe, 118
unten: down, 126b, downstairs, 6
unter: under, 126a
Unterführung: underpass, 37
Unterhaltungsserie: comedy, 101
Unterhemd: vest, 9
Unterhosen: pants, 12
unterirdischer See: underground lake, 110
unterrichten: teach, taught, taught, 124d
Unterrock: petticoat, 9, slip, 9
Unterseite: bottom, 25
Uranus: Uranus, 118
Uruguay: Uruguay, 115

V

Vaduz: Vaduz, 112
Vaiaku: Vaiaku, 116
Valboe District: Valboe District, 116
Valletta: Valletta, 112
Vanuatu: Vanuatu, 116
Vasall: vassal, 84
Vasen: vases, 80
Vater: father, 5
Veilchen: violet, 70
Venen: veins, 2
Venezuela: Venezuela, 115
Venus: Venus, 118
Verband: bandage, 53
Verben: verbs, 124a, 124b, 124c, 124d
Verbrennungsofen: incinerator, 106

Verdauung: digestion, 2
Vereinigte Arabische Emirate: United Arab
Emirates, 113
Vereinigte Staaten von Amerika: United
States of America, 115
Vereinigtes Königreich: United
Kingdom, 112
Vergißmeinnicht: forget-me-not, 70
Vergrößerungsglas: magnifying
glass, 54, 61
verkaufen: sell, sold, sold, 124d
Verkäufer: shop assistant, 34, 59b
Verkäuferin: sales girl, 36
Verkehr: traffic, 30
Verkehrspolizist: traffic policeman on
point duty, 30
Verkehrszeichen: traffic signs, 37, 38
Verlängerungskabel: extension lead, 65
Verlies: dungeon, 84
der verrückte Hutmacher: Mad Hatter, 91
Versammlung: assembly, 22
Versammlungsplatz: agora, 82
Verschlußmechanismus: shutter
mechanism, 61
Verschlußzeitregler: shutter speed
control, 68
Verstärker: amplifier, 100, 101
verstellbarer Schraubenschlüssel:
adjustable spanner, 63, 64
Verteidigung: defence, 55
Verzeichnis: register, 48
Victoria: Victoria, 114
Victoria-Fälle: Victoria Falls, 114
Videokassette: videotape, 101
Videorecorder: video tape recorder, 101,
videorecorder, 11
Viehwagen: cattle train, 42
Vientiane: Vientiane, 113
vier: four, 23
vierte/r: fourth, 23
viertel nach sechs: quarter past six, 56
viertel vor elf: quarter to eleven, 56
vierzehn: fourteen, 23
vierzig: forty, 23
Vietnam: Vietnam, 113
Viola: viola, 99
violett: purple, 26
Violine: violin, 99
Viper: viper, 74
Vogelscheuche: scarecrow, 107
voll: full, 125b
Volleyball: volley ball, 122
Vollkornbrot: wholemeal bread, 33
Vollmond: full moon, 118
von (weg): off, 126b
von: from, 126b
vor: in front of, 126a
Vorbackenzähne: premolar teeth, 62
Vorbohrer: gimlet, 63
vordere Beifahrertür: front passenger
door, 44
vordere Fußraste: front foot-rest, 40
Vorderradbremshebel: front-wheel
brake, 40
Vorderseite: front, 25
Vorfahrt beachten: junction ahead, 38
Vorfeld der Flughalle: apron, 45
Vorführraum: projection room, 102
Vorgeschichte: prehistory, 80
Vorhang: curtain, 11, 13, 102
Vororte: outskirts of town, 106
Vorrat an Obst und Gemüse: supply of
fruits and vegetables, 31

Vorratslager: storerooms, 84
vorwärts: forward, 101
Vulkan: volcano, 111
Vulkanausbruch: eruption, 110
Vulkankrater: volcanic crater, 110

W

Waage: Libra, the balance, 117, scales, 10,
28, 34, 49
Waagschale: pan, 28
Wachturm: watchtower, 84
Wagen: carriage, 43, waggon, 87
Wagenheber: jack, 39
Wagenlenker: charioteers, 83
Wählscheibe: dial, 8, 49
Wal: hale, 78
Wald: forest, 76, 111, 112, 115, wood, 109, 112
Waldhorn: French horn, 99
Walkie-Talkie: walkie-talkie, 92
Walroß: walrus, 78
Wand: wall, 11, 14, 126a
Wange: cheek, 2
Warschau: Warsaw, 112
warten: wait, waited, waited, 124d
Wärter: warder, 54
Warteraum: waiting-room, 43, 45
Waschbecken: sink, 7, washbasin, 10
Wäscheklammer: peg, 6
Wäschekorb: laundry-basket, 10
Wäscheleine: washing line, 6
waschen: wash, washed, washed, 124b
Waschmaschine: washing machine, 7
wäscht: does the washing, 66
Washington: Washington, 115
Wasser: water, 17, 52
Wasserball: water polo, 96
Wasserbehälter: water carriers, 105
Wasserfall: waterfall, 109
Wasserfarben: water colours, 60
Wasserhahn: (water) tap, 64
Wasserhähne: taps, 7
Wasserkasten: toilet cistern, 64
Wassermann: Aquarius, the water
carrier, 117
Wassermelonen: watermelons, 32
Wasserschlauch: watering-pipe, 6
Wasserski: water skiing, 96
Wasserspeier: gargoyle, 85
Wassersport: aquatic sports, 96
Wassertank: water tank, 42
Wasserwaage: level, 63
Watte: cotton-wool, 53
WC: toilet, 10
Wecker: alarm clock, 13, 56
Wegweiser: signpost, 30
weich: soft, 125b
Weide: willow, 71
Weihnachten: Christmas, 18
Weihnachtsbaum: Christmas tree, 18, 57
Weihnachtskarte: Christmas card, 18
Weihnachtskuchen: Christmas cake, 18
Weihnachtsmann: Father Christmas, 18
Weihnachtstag, 1.: Christmas Day, 18
Weihnachtstag, 2.: Boxing Day, 18
Wein: wine, 16, 17
Weinbrand: brandy, 35
weinen: cry, cried, cried, 124b
weiß: white, 26

SOLUTIONS

That's me: 15 - 13 - 12 - 6 - 5 - 18 - 3 - 7 - 11 - 10 - 1 - 9 - 8 - 2 - 4 - 17 - 13 - 14

Sums:

Find the words: eyes - face - leg - nose - chest - knee - chini - foot - thumb - stomach

Colours: 1, green - 2, red - 3, yellow - 4, orange - 5, white - 6, blue - 7, pink

Verbs maze: laugh - eat - look for - study - wash

Hidden namens: Martin - Sandra - James - Marcello - Caroline - Stephen

Opposites:

1, good - 2, large - 3, long - 4, old - 5, bad - 6, short - 7, new - 8, small

What's the weather like today?: cloudy - raining - snowing - sunny - windy - freezing - hot - warm - cold - foggy - wet - thundering and lighting